DIABETIC
COOKBOOK
FOR BEGINNERS

Embark on a flavorful journey to better health with our

Diabetic Cookbook for Beginners – your trusted companion

in transforming your meals and managing diabetes with ease and delight!

AUTHOR NAME

CONTENTS

INTRODUCTION

Welcome to the "Diabetic Cookbook for Beginners," where every recipe is more than just a meal; it's a step towards a healthier, more vibrant you. We understand that being diagnosed with diabetes can feel overwhelming, but you're not alone. This cookbook is designed to be your friendly guide in the kitchen, offering delicious and nutritious recipes that cater to your dietary needs.

Our primary goal is to inspire and empower you to take control of your health through what you eat. We believe that a diabetic-friendly diet should not be bland or restrictive. Instead, it can be an exciting exploration of flavors and ingredients that satisfy your taste buds and keep your blood sugar levels in check.

We've carefully curated a selection of easy-to-follow recipes using accessible and beneficial ingredients for managing diabetes. From hearty breakfasts to delectable desserts, we aim to provide a variety of options to suit your preferences and lifestyle.

So, whether you're newly diagnosed or looking to refresh your meal plan, this cookbook supports you on your journey to better health. Let's embrace the joy of cooking and turn every meal into an opportunity to nourish your body and soul. Welcome to a world of flavorful possibilities!

CHAPTER 1: UNDERSTANDING DIABETES

Diabetes is a chronic condition affecting how your body processes blood sugar, or glucose, which is vital for energy production. There are three main types of diabetes: Type 1, Type 2, and gestational diabetes. Type 1 diabetes is an autoimmune condition where the body's immune system attacks insulin-producing cells, leading to insulin deficiency. Type 2 diabetes, the most common form, occurs when the body becomes resistant to insulin or doesn't produce enough of it. Gestational diabetes develops during pregnancy and usually resolves after childbirth, but it increases the risk of developing Type 2 diabetes later in life.

In the United States, diabetes is a significant health concern. According to the Centers for Disease Control and Prevention (CDC), over 37 million Americans have diabetes, and 1 in 5 of them are unaware of their condition. Additionally, more than 96 million adults have prediabetes, a condition characterized by higher-than-normal blood sugar levels that can lead to Type 2 diabetes if not managed properly.

SYMPTOMS AND DIAGNOSIS

Recognizing the symptoms of diabetes is crucial for early detection and management. Common signs include:

- **Frequent urination:** An increased need to urinate, often at night.
- **Excessive thirst:** Feeling unusually thirsty despite drinking plenty of fluids.
- **Unexplained weight loss:** Losing weight without trying, especially in Type 1 diabetes.
- **Fatigue:** Feeling unusually tired or lethargic.
- **Blurred vision:** Experiencing changes in vision or clarity.
- **Slow-healing sores or cuts:** Wounds that take longer to heal than usual.

If you experience any of these symptoms, it's important to consult a healthcare professional. Diagnosis typically involves a series of blood tests:

- **A1C test:** Measures average blood sugar levels over the past two to three months. A result of 6.5% or higher indicates diabetes.
- **Fasting plasma glucose test:** Checks blood sugar levels after an overnight fast. A result of 126 mg/dL or higher suggests diabetes.
- **Oral glucose tolerance test:** Measures blood sugar before and two hours after consuming a sugary drink. A two-hour level of 200 mg/dL or higher indicates diabetes.

RISK FACTORS

Several factors can increase your risk of developing diabetes:

- **Genetics and family history:** Having a close relative with diabetes increases your risk.
- **Weight:** Being overweight or obese is a major risk factor for Type 2 diabetes.

- **Age:** The risk of Type 2 diabetes increases with age, particularly after 45 years.
- **Sedentary lifestyle:** Lack of physical activity can increase the risk.
- **Ethnicity:** Certain ethnic groups, including African Americans, Hispanic/Latino Americans, American Indians, and Asian Americans, are at higher risk.
- **Gestational diabetes:** Women who have had gestational diabetes are at higher risk of developing Type 2 diabetes later in life.
- **Polycystic ovary syndrome (PCOS):** Women with PCOS are at increased risk.

Understanding these risk factors can help individuals take preventive measures to reduce their risk or manage the condition effectively if diagnosed.

LONG-TERM COMPLICATIONS

Uncontrolled diabetes can lead to a range of long-term complications that affect various parts of the body. These complications arise from prolonged high blood sugar levels, which can damage blood vessels and nerves. Some of the potential complications include:

- **Heart disease:** People with diabetes are at a higher risk of developing heart disease, including coronary artery disease, heart attack, and stroke.
- **Kidney damage (nephropathy):** Diabetes can lead to kidney disease, which may progress to kidney failure if not managed properly.
- **Vision problems:** Diabetic retinopathy, cataracts, and glaucoma are more common in individuals with diabetes, potentially leading to blindness.
- **Nerve damage (neuropathy):** High blood sugar can damage nerves, leading to numbness, tingling, and pain, particularly in the hands and feet.
- **Foot problems:** Nerve damage and poor circulation in the feet can lead to serious infections and possibly amputation.

Early detection and effective management of diabetes are crucial to prevent or delay the onset of these complications.

DIABETES MANAGEMENT

Managing diabetes effectively requires a comprehensive approach that includes regular monitoring of blood glucose levels, adherence to dietary guidelines, and an active lifestyle. Key components of diabetes management include:

- **Blood glucose monitoring:** Regularly checking blood sugar levels helps individuals make informed decisions about their diet, exercise, and medication.
- **Dietary guidelines:** Eating a balanced diet with controlled portions of carbohydrates, lean proteins, and healthy fats is essential. Incorporating fiber-rich foods and monitoring carbohydrate intake can help stabilize blood sugar levels.
- **Exercise:** Regular physical activity helps control blood sugar levels, improve insulin sensitivity, and reduce the risk of heart disease.

- **Medication:** For some individuals, medication or insulin therapy may be necessary to manage blood sugar levels effectively.

Working closely with a healthcare team is crucial to tailor a diabetes management plan that meets individual needs.

SUPPORT AND RESOURCES

Living with diabetes can be a challenging journey, but you don't have to navigate it alone. Seeking support from various sources can provide you with valuable information, encouragement, and a sense of community. Here are some ways to find support and resources:

- **Healthcare Professionals:** Building a strong relationship with your healthcare team, including your primary care physician, endocrinologist, and diabetes educator, is crucial. They can provide personalized advice, help you monitor your progress, and adjust your treatment plan as needed.
- **Support Groups:** Joining a diabetes support group can be incredibly beneficial. These groups offer a platform to share experiences, tips, and coping strategies with others who understand what you're going through. You can find local support groups through hospitals, community centers, or online platforms.
- **Online Communities:** The internet is a valuable resource for finding support and information. Websites, forums, and social media groups dedicated to diabetes can offer advice, recipes, and motivation. Just be sure to verify the credibility of the sources.
- **Educational Resources:** Educating yourself about diabetes is key to effective management. Reputable organizations like the American Diabetes Association (ADA) and the National Institute of Diabetes and Digestive and Kidney Diseases (NIDDK) offer a wealth of information on their websites, including guides on nutrition, exercise, and medication.
- **Nutritionists and Dietitians:** Consulting with a registered dietitian or nutritionist who specializes in diabetes can help you develop a meal plan that suits your individual needs and preferences.
- **Mental Health Support:** Managing diabetes can be emotionally taxing. If you're feeling overwhelmed, consider seeking support from a mental health professional who can help you cope with stress, anxiety, or depression.

REPUTABLE ORGANIZATIONS FOR MORE INFORMATION

- **American Diabetes Association (ADA):** A leading organization dedicated to diabetes research, advocacy, and education. Their website provides comprehensive information on diabetes management, including dietary guidelines and lifestyle tips.
- **Centers for Disease Control and Prevention (CDC) - Diabetes:** Offers a wide range of resources, including statistics, prevention strategies, and management tips.
- **National Diabetes Education Program (NDEP):** A partnership between the National Institutes of Health (NIH) and the CDC, providing resources for diabetes prevention and control.

Remember, seeking support is a sign of strength. By leveraging these resources, you can gain the knowledge, skills, and confidence needed to manage your diabetes effectively and live a healthy, fulfilling life.

CHAPTER 2: PRINCIPLES OF A DIABETIC DIET

A diabetic diet is not just about managing blood sugar levels; it's about creating a balanced and nutritious meal plan that supports overall health. The key principles of a diabetic diet involve understanding how different foods affect your blood sugar and making informed choices to maintain stable glucose levels. This chapter will guide you through the fundamentals of macronutrient balancing and the significance of the glycemic index in a diabetic diet.

MACRONUTRIENT BALANCING

Managing diabetes effectively requires a deep understanding of how macronutrients - carbohydrates, proteins, and fats - influence blood glucose levels. Here's a closer look at each macronutrient and tips for achieving a balanced intake:

Carbohydrates: Carbohydrates are the primary source of energy for the body, but they also have the most significant impact on blood sugar levels. They are found in foods like fruits, vegetables, grains, and dairy products. For optimal glucose control, focus on consuming complex carbohydrates, which are high in fiber and digest more slowly, leading to a gradual rise in blood sugar. Examples include whole grains, legumes, and non-starchy vegetables. Aim to distribute your carbohydrate intake evenly throughout the day to prevent spikes in blood sugar.

Proteins: Proteins are crucial for building and repairing tissues, and they have a minimal effect on blood glucose levels. Including a source of lean protein in each meal can help stabilize blood sugar by slowing the absorption of carbohydrates. Good sources of lean protein include poultry, fish, tofu, legumes, and low-fat dairy products. Proteins can also increase feelings of fullness, which can help with weight management.

Fats: While fats have little direct impact on blood sugar levels, they are an essential part of a healthy diet. Healthy fats can slow the digestion of carbohydrates, contributing to more stable blood sugar levels. Focus on incorporating unsaturated fats, such as those found in avocados, nuts, seeds, and olive oil, into your meals. Limit the intake of saturated and trans fats, which can increase the risk of heart disease.

To balance macronutrients in each meal:

Plate Method: Use the plate method as a guide for meal planning. Fill half of your plate with non-starchy vegetables, one-quarter with lean protein, and one-quarter with whole grains or starchy vegetables.

Portion Control: Be mindful of portion sizes, especially for carbohydrate-rich foods. Use measuring cups or a food scale to ensure accurate portions.

Meal Timing: Eat regular meals and snacks throughout the day to maintain steady blood sugar levels. Avoid skipping meals, which can lead to overeating or spikes in blood sugar.

By understanding and balancing the macronutrients in your diet, you can better manage your blood glucose levels and overall health.

THE IMPORTANCE OF THE GLYCEMIC INDEX

The glycemic index (GI) is a valuable tool in managing diabetes, as it measures how quickly a carbohydrate-containing food raises blood glucose levels. Foods are ranked on a scale from 0 to 100, with higher scores indicating a faster increase in blood sugar. Understanding the GI can help you make informed choices about what to eat to maintain stable blood glucose levels.

Low GI Foods (55 or less): These foods cause a slow and steady rise in blood sugar, making them ideal for diabetes management. Examples include most non-starchy vegetables, some fruits (like apples and oranges), legumes (beans, lentils), and whole grains (barley, quinoa).

Medium GI Foods (56-69): These foods cause a moderate increase in blood sugar. Examples include some fruits (like pineapple and melon), sweet potatoes, and whole wheat products.

High GI Foods (70 or more): These foods cause a rapid spike in blood sugar and should be consumed sparingly. Examples include white bread, white rice, and sugary snacks.

Tips for Incorporating Low-GI Foods into Your Diet:

- **Choose Whole Grains:** opt for whole grain bread, pasta, and cereals instead of their refined counterparts. Whole grains have a lower GI and provide more fiber and nutrients.
- **Include Legumes:** Incorporate beans, lentils, and chickpeas into your meals. They are low in GI and high in protein and fiber.
- **Eat More Non-Starchy Vegetables:** Fill your plate with vegetables like broccoli, spinach, and carrots. They are low in calories and GI, and rich in vitamins and minerals.
- **Select Low-GI Fruits:** Choose fruits such as berries, cherries, and apples. Pairing fruit with a protein source, like yogurt or nuts, can also help minimize blood sugar spikes.
- **Limit Sugary and Processed Foods:** Avoid foods high in added sugars and refined carbohydrates, as they tend to have a high GI.
- **Balance Your Meals:** Combine low-GI foods with moderate amounts of protein and healthy fats to create balanced meals that support stable blood sugar levels.

CARBOHYDRATES AND DIABETES CONTROL

Carbohydrates play a pivotal role in diabetes management, as they directly impact blood glucose levels. Understanding the quantity and quality of carbohydrates you consume can help you maintain better control over your diabetes.

Quantity of Carbohydrates: Monitoring the amount of carbohydrates in each meal is crucial for keeping blood sugar levels within the target range. This is often referred to as carbohydrate counting or carb counting. It involves calculating the total grams of carbohydrates in your meal and adjusting your medication or insulin dose accordingly. The American Diabetes Association recommends starting with a daily intake of 45-60 grams of carbohydrates per meal, but individual needs may vary.

Quality of Carbohydrates: Not all carbohydrates are created equal. The quality of carbohydrates you choose is just as important as the quantity. Complex carbohydrates, such as whole grains, legumes, and vegetables, are preferred over simple carbohydrates found in sugary snacks and processed foods. Complex carbs are high in fiber, which slows down digestion and absorption, leading to a more gradual rise in blood sugar levels.

Tips for Reading Food Labels for Better Carbohydrate Selection:

- **Check the Serving Size:** Always compare the serving size on the label to the amount you're actually consuming. This will help you accurately calculate the total carbohydrates.
- **Look at Total Carbohydrates:** Pay attention to the total carbohydrates, which include sugars, starches, and fiber.
- **Consider the Fiber Content:** High-fiber foods can have a less significant impact on blood sugar. Subtract the grams of fiber from the total carbohydrates for a more accurate carb count.
- **Watch for Added Sugars:** Look for terms like "sucrose," "high-fructose corn syrup," or "dextrose" in the ingredients list. Minimize foods with added sugars, as they can cause rapid spikes in blood glucose.
- **Use the Glycemic Index:** Choose foods with a lower glycemic index (GI) for a slower, more stable blood sugar response.

DIETARY FIBER: YOUR ALLY AGAINST DIABETES

Dietary fiber is a powerful tool in the management of diabetes. It's the indigestible part of plant foods that can have a profound impact on your health, especially when it comes to controlling blood glucose levels. Here's why fiber is so beneficial for diabetics and some fiber-rich foods to include in your diet.

Benefits of Fiber in the Diabetic Diet:

- **Improves Glucose Control:** Fiber slows down the absorption of sugar in the bloodstream, helping to prevent rapid spikes in blood glucose levels.
- **Increases Satiety:** Fiber-rich foods tend to be more filling, which can help you eat less and manage your weight— a crucial aspect of diabetes management.
- **Lowers Cholesterol:** Soluble fiber can help lower LDL ("bad") cholesterol levels, reducing the risk of heart disease, a common concern for people with diabetes.
- **Supports Digestive Health:** Fiber aids in digestion and helps prevent constipation, a common problem for many diabetics.

Fiber-Rich Sources Recommended for Diabetics:

- **Legumes:** Beans, lentils, and chickpeas are excellent sources of fiber and protein, making them a great choice for blood sugar control.
- **Whole Grains:** opt for whole grain bread, brown rice, quinoa, and oats instead of refined grains. These are higher in fiber and nutrients.
- **Vegetables:** Non-starchy vegetables like broccoli, spinach, and carrots are low in calories and high in fiber, making them ideal for a diabetic diet.

- **Fruits:** While fruits contain natural sugars, they are also rich in fiber. Berries, apples, and pears with the skin on are good choices.
- **Nuts and Seeds:** Almonds, chia seeds, and flaxseeds are not only high in fiber but also healthy fats that can help manage blood sugar levels.

When increasing your fiber intake, do so gradually to avoid digestive discomfort, and be sure to drink plenty of water. Incorporating a variety of fiber-rich foods into your diet can help you manage your diabetes more effectively and improve your overall health.

HEALTHY FATS AND DIET FOR DIABETICS

Fats are an essential part of a balanced diet, even for individuals with diabetes. However, not all fats are created equal. Understanding the difference between "good" and "bad" fats and their impact on diabetic health is crucial for managing your condition effectively.

"Good" Fats:

- **Monounsaturated Fats:** These fats can help reduce bad cholesterol levels and lower the risk of heart disease, a common concern for diabetics. They are found in foods like olive oil, avocados, and nuts.
- **Polyunsaturated Fats:** Including omega-3 and omega-6 fatty acids, these fats are essential for brain function and cell growth. Omega-3s, in particular, have been shown to decrease the risk of heart disease. Good sources include fatty fish like salmon, walnuts, and flaxseeds.

"Bad" Fats:

- **Saturated Fats:** Found in animal products like red meat, butter, and cheese, saturated fats can raise your cholesterol levels and increase the risk of heart disease. It's advisable to limit their intake.
- **Trans Fats:** Often found in processed foods, baked goods, and fried foods, trans fats are the worst type of fat for your health. They raise bad cholesterol levels and lower good cholesterol, increasing the risk of heart disease. Avoid them as much as possible.

Examples of Healthy Fat Sources for Diabetics:

- **Avocados:** Rich in monounsaturated fats, avocados can help improve cholesterol levels and decrease the risk of heart disease.
- **Nuts and Seeds:** Almonds, walnuts, chia seeds, and flaxseeds are great sources of healthy fats and can be a nutritious snack or addition to meals.
- **Olive Oil:** Olive oil is high in monounsaturated fats and has anti-inflammatory properties. It can be used for cooking or as a salad dressing.
- **Fatty Fish:** Salmon, mackerel, and sardines are high in omega-3 fatty acids, which are beneficial for heart health.

MEAL TRACKING AND PLANNING

Effective diabetes management relies heavily on consistent meal tracking and planning. By keeping a close eye on what and when you eat, you can maintain better control over your blood glucose levels and overall health.

Techniques to Monitor Food Intake:

- **Food Diary:** Keep a daily record of everything you eat and drink, including portion sizes and carbohydrate content. This can help you identify patterns and make necessary adjustments to your diet.
- **Carbohydrate Counting:** Learn to count the grams of carbohydrates in your meals and snacks. This is essential for determining how much insulin you may need if you're on insulin therapy.
- **Use Technology:** There are numerous apps and online tools available to help you track your food intake, monitor your blood sugar levels, and plan your meals.

Planning Meals in Advance:

- **Create a Meal Plan:** Plan your meals and snacks for the week ahead. This can help you ensure a balanced diet and prevent impulsive, unhealthy food choices.
- **Prepare Meals in Bulk:** Cooking in bulk and storing portions for later can save time and make it easier to stick to your meal plan.
- **Include a Variety of Foods:** Make sure your meal plan includes a balance of carbohydrates, proteins, and healthy fats, along with plenty of fiber-rich fruits and vegetables.

Consistency in Mealtimes:

- **Regular Eating Schedule:** Try to eat your meals and snacks at the same times each day. This can help keep your blood sugar levels stable throughout the day.
- **Avoid Skipping Meals:** Skipping meals can lead to fluctuations in blood sugar levels and may increase the risk of overeating later.

By implementing this meal tracking and planning techniques, you can take an active role in managing your diabetes and maintaining a healthy lifestyle.

HYDRATION AND DIABETES MANAGEMENT

Hydration plays a crucial role in diabetes management. Water is essential for various bodily functions, including regulating blood sugar levels and ensuring the proper functioning of the kidneys, which are often affected by diabetes.

Role of Water in Diabetes Management:

- **Blood Sugar Control:** Proper hydration helps maintain normal blood sugar levels. Dehydration can cause blood sugar to become concentrated, leading to hyperglycemia.
- **Kidney Health:** Diabetes can put a strain on the kidneys, which are responsible for filtering waste from the blood. Staying hydrated helps the kidneys function efficiently and reduces the risk of kidney-related complications.
- **Appetite Control:** Drinking water can help you feel full, which can be beneficial in managing weight and reducing the likelihood of overeating.

Advice on Increasing Fluid Intake:

- **Set Daily Goals:** Aim for at least 8-10 cups of water a day, but individual needs may vary depending on factors such as activity level and climate.

- **Carry a Water Bottle:** Carrying a water bottle throughout the day can remind you to drink regularly.
- **Drink Before You Feel Thirsty:** Thirst is often a late sign of dehydration. Sip water throughout the day to stay ahead of your thirst.
- **Incorporate Water-Rich Foods:** Fruits and vegetables with high water content, such as cucumbers, watermelon, and oranges, can help keep you hydrated.

What Drinks to Avoid:

- **Sugary Drinks:** Soda, fruit juices, and sweetened beverages can cause spikes in blood sugar levels and should be avoided or consumed in moderation.
- **Alcoholic Beverages:** Alcohol can lead to dehydration and affect blood sugar levels. If you choose to drink, do so in moderation and with a meal.
- **Caffeinated Drinks:** While moderate amounts of coffee and tea can be part of a healthy diet, excessive caffeine can lead to dehydration.

Staying hydrated is a simple yet effective aspect of diabetes management. By prioritizing water intake and making smart beverage choices, you can support your overall health and well-being.

CHAPTER 3: RECOMMENDED AND AVOIDED FOODS

Managing diabetes effectively involves making informed choices about what you eat. Certain foods can help stabilize blood sugar levels, while others may cause them to spike. In this chapter, we'll explore diabetic-friendly foods that can be incorporated into your diet and those that are best avoided.

DIABETIC FRIENDLY FOODS

Leafy Greens: Packed with essential vitamins and minerals, leafy greens like spinach, kale, and collard greens are low in calories and carbohydrates, making them ideal for blood sugar control. Their high antioxidant content can also help reduce inflammation and protect against diabetes-related complications.

Whole Grains: Unlike refined grains, whole grains like quinoa, brown rice, and oats retain their fiber and nutrient content. The fiber in whole grains slows down digestion, preventing rapid spikes in blood sugar levels.

Legumes: Beans, lentils, and chickpeas are excellent sources of plant-based protein and fiber. They can help regulate blood sugar levels, improve cholesterol levels, and keep you feeling full and satisfied.

Low-GI Fruits: While fruits are an important part of a balanced diet, choosing low-glycemic index (GI) options like berries, cherries, and apples can help minimize blood sugar spikes. Be mindful of portion sizes, as overeating fruit can still affect blood sugar levels.

Lean Proteins: Incorporating lean proteins into your meals can help stabilize blood sugar levels and promote satiety. Opt for sources like chicken breast, turkey, fish, tofu, and eggs. Plant-based protein sources like legumes and quinoa are also excellent choices.

Healthy Fats: Monounsaturated and polyunsaturated fats found in olive oil, avocados, nuts, and seeds can help improve insulin sensitivity and reduce the risk of heart disease. Including moderate amounts of these healthy fats in your diet can support overall health and diabetes management.

In addition to these diabetic-friendly foods, it's important to stay hydrated and limit your intake of added sugars, refined carbohydrates, and processed foods. By focusing on whole, nutrient-rich foods, you can create a balanced diet that supports your diabetes management and overall well-being.

FOODS TO LIMIT OR AVOID

While a diabetic-friendly diet includes a variety of nutritious foods, certain items should be limited or avoided to maintain optimal blood sugar control and overall health.

Simple Sugars and Artificial Sweeteners: Foods and beverages high in simple sugars, such as candy, soda, and desserts, can cause rapid spikes in blood glucose levels. While artificial sweeteners may not directly affect blood sugar, some studies suggest they could potentially impact insulin sensitivity and appetite regulation. It's best to limit these sweeteners and opt for natural sources of sweetness, like fruits, in moderation.

Highly Processed Foods: Processed foods often contain added sugars, unhealthy fats, and high levels of sodium, which can negatively affect blood sugar levels and overall health. Examples include fast food, packaged snacks, and processed meats. Healthier alternatives include whole, minimally processed foods like fresh fruits and vegetables, lean proteins, and whole grains.

Saturated and Trans Fats: These unhealthy fats are found in foods like fatty cuts of meat, full-fat dairy products, and many baked goods. They can contribute to insulin resistance and increase the risk of heart disease, which is already higher in individuals with diabetes. Opt for healthier fats, such as those found in avocados, nuts, seeds, and olive oil.

Alcohol: While moderate alcohol consumption may be safe for some people with diabetes, it's important to be cautious. Alcohol can interfere with blood sugar control and medication effectiveness. If you choose to drink, do so in moderation (up to one drink per day for women and up to two drinks per day for men) and always with food to prevent hypoglycemia.

By being mindful of these foods and making informed choices, you can better manage your diabetes and support your overall health.

SMART REPLACEMENTS

Making smart food swaps can help you manage diabetes without feeling deprived. Here are some ideas for healthier alternatives to satisfy cravings and improve your overall diet.

Sweets and Snacks:

- **Fruit:** Satisfy your sweet tooth with fresh, frozen, or dried fruits. Berries, apples, and pears are excellent choices.
- **Dark Chocolate:** Opt for a small piece of dark chocolate (at least 70% cocoa) instead of milk chocolate or candy bars.
- **Yogurt:** Choose plain Greek yogurt and sweeten it with a touch of honey or fresh fruit instead of flavored yogurts high in added sugars.
- **Nuts:** Instead of chips or crackers, snack on a handful of unsalted nuts like almonds, walnuts, or pistachios.

Drinks:

- **Water:** Stay hydrated with water instead of sugary sodas or juices. Add a slice of lemon, lime, or cucumber for a refreshing twist.
- **Herbal Tea:** Enjoy unsweetened herbal teas as a calorie-free alternative to sweetened beverages.
- **Coffee:** If you drink coffee, opt for black coffee, or use a small amount of milk or a milk alternative without added sugars.

Flours and Cereals:

- **Whole Wheat Flour:** Replace white flour with whole wheat flour in baking recipes to increase fiber content.

- **Oat Flour:** For a gluten-free option, try oat flour in your baking recipes. It adds a mild, nutty flavor and is rich in fiber.
- **Whole Grain Cereals:** Choose cereals made from whole grains like oats, barley, or quinoa. Look for options with minimal added sugars and at least 3 grams of fiber per serving.

By making these smart replacements, you can enjoy a varied and delicious diet while keeping your blood sugar levels in check.

READ FOOD LABELS

Understanding food labels is a vital skill for managing diabetes. Knowing what to look for can help you make healthier choices and control your blood sugar levels.

What to Look For:

- **Serving Size:** Check the serving size and compare it to how much you actually eat. The nutrition information on the label is based on this amount.
- **Total Carbohydrates:** Look at the total carbohydrates, which include sugars, starches, and fiber. This number is crucial for managing your blood sugar.
- **Fiber:** High-fiber foods can help control blood sugar levels. Aim for foods with at least 3 grams of fiber per serving.
- **Sugars:** Pay attention to the amount of sugar, especially added sugars. Foods with high sugar content can cause spikes in blood sugar.
- **Protein:** Protein is important for blood sugar management and overall health. Choose foods with a good amount of protein.
- **Fat:** Look for foods with healthy fats, such as monounsaturated and polyunsaturated fats. Avoid trans fats and limit saturated fats.
- **Calculating Net Carbs:** Net carbs are the carbohydrates that affect blood sugar levels. They are calculated by subtracting fiber and sugar alcohols from the total carbohydrates. Here's how to do it:
- **Find the Total Carbohydrates:** Look for the total carbohydrates on the nutrition label.
- **Subtract Fiber:** If the food has fiber, subtract the grams of fiber from the total carbohydrates. Fiber doesn't significantly affect blood sugar levels.
- **Subtract Sugar Alcohols (if applicable):** If the product contains sugar alcohols (like xylitol or erythritol), you can subtract half of the grams of sugar alcohols from the total carbohydrates.

The result is the net carbs, which gives you a better idea of how the food will impact your blood sugar levels.

Understanding and using food labels can empower you to make informed choices about what you eat. By focusing on net carbs, fiber, and avoiding added sugars, you can manage your diabetes more effectively and maintain a balanced diet.

SHOPPING TIPS

Creating a diabetic-friendly shopping list and developing smart shopping strategies are essential steps in managing your diabetes through diet. Here are some tips to help you navigate the supermarket and make informed food choices.

Diabetic Shopping List:

A well-planned shopping list can help you focus on buying diabetes-friendly foods and avoid impulse purchases. Here's a basic list to get you started:

- **Vegetables:** Stock up on non-starchy vegetables like spinach, kale, bell peppers, broccoli, and cauliflower. They are low in carbs and high in fiber and nutrients.
- **Fruits:** Choose low-glycemic index fruits such as berries, cherries, apples, and pears. Be mindful of portion sizes to manage your carb intake.
- **Whole Grains:** Look for whole grains like quinoa, brown rice, barley, and whole wheat pasta. They provide fiber and nutrients that are stripped from refined grains.
- **Legumes:** Beans, lentils, and chickpeas are great sources of plant-based protein and fiber, making them excellent choices for a diabetic diet.
- **Lean Proteins:** Include lean protein sources like skinless poultry, fish, tofu, and eggs. They help keep you full and stabilize blood sugar levels.
- **Healthy Fats:** Avocados, nuts, seeds, and olive oil are sources of healthy fats that can improve heart health and satiety.
- **Dairy:** Opt for low-fat or non-fat dairy products like milk, yogurt, and cheese to reduce your intake of saturated fat.

Shopping Strategies:

- **Stick to the Perimeter:** The outer aisles of the supermarket typically contain fresh foods like fruits, vegetables, and lean proteins. The inner aisles often have more processed and high-sugar foods.
- **Read Labels:** Always read nutrition labels to check for added sugars, unhealthy fats, and overall carbohydrate content. Look for foods with minimal ingredients and low sodium.
- **Plan Ahead:** Create a meal plan for the week and make a shopping list based on your plan. This can help you stay focused and avoid buying unhealthy foods on impulse.
- **Don't Shop Hungry:** Shopping on an empty stomach can lead to impulse purchases of high-carb or sugary snacks. Eat a healthy snack before you go to the store.
- **Choose Frozen or Canned:** If fresh produce is not available or too expensive, frozen or canned fruits and vegetables can be good alternatives. Just make sure they don't have added sugars or sodium.
- **Buy in Bulk:** Purchasing non-perishable items like whole grains and legumes in bulk can save money and ensure you have diabetes-friendly staples on hand.

By following these shopping tips and keeping a well-stocked kitchen, you can make it easier to prepare healthy, diabetes-friendly meals at home.

Here is a summary table of foods to prefer and those to avoid for a balanced diet in diabetes management:

Foods to Prefer	Foods to Avoid
Leafy greens (spinach, kale, lettuce)	Simple sugars (sweets, sugary drinks)
Whole grains (oats, quinoa, brown rice)	Processed foods (packaged snacks, ready-to-eat meals)
Legumes (beans, lentils, chickpeas)	Saturated and trans fats (fried foods, fast food)
Low GI fruits (apples, pears, berries)	Refined carbohydrates (white bread, white pasta)
Lean protein (skinless chicken, fish, tofu)	Alcoholic beverages (excessive consumption)
Healthy fats (olive oil, nuts, avocados)	Red and processed meats (sausages, bacon)
Low-fat dairy products (Greek yogurt, milk)	Salad food and snack salad (chips, pretzel)
Water and unsweetened beverages (naturally flavored water, sugar-free tea)	Artificial sweeteners (in diet products, they can affect blood sugar)

CHAPTER 4: MEAL PLANNING AND PORTION CONTROL

Managing diabetes effectively requires careful attention to both what you eat and how much you eat. This chapter will guide you through the essentials of meal planning and portion control, two key strategies for maintaining stable blood glucose levels and achieving a healthy weight.

THE IMPORTANCE OF MEAL PLANNING

Meal planning is a powerful tool in diabetes management. It involves deciding in advance what you will eat for your meals and snacks. This proactive approach can help you:

- **Maintain Stable Blood Glucose Levels:** By planning balanced meals with the right mix of carbohydrates, proteins, and fats, you can prevent sudden spikes or drops in blood sugar.
- **Control Portions:** Planning helps you determine the appropriate portion sizes for your meals, which is crucial for managing your calorie intake and blood sugar.
- **Reduce Stress:** Knowing what you're going to eat ahead of time can reduce the stress of last-minute decisions and help you avoid unhealthy choices.
- **Save Time and Money:** Planning and preparing meals in advance can save time during the week and help you avoid expensive and unhealthy takeout options.

Tips for Meal Planning:

- **Start with a Template:** Create a basic template for your meals, ensuring each one includes a source of protein, healthy fats, and fiber-rich carbohydrates.
- **Prepare in Advance:** Set aside time each week to prepare meals or meal components in advance. This can include chopping vegetables, cooking grains, or portioning out snacks.
- **Be Flexible:** While it's good to have a plan, be flexible enough to adjust it based on your schedule, cravings, or changes in your blood sugar levels.
- **Use Technology:** There are many apps and online tools available that can help you plan your meals and track your nutritional intake.

PRINCIPLES OF PORTION CONTROL

Portion control is a cornerstone of effective diabetes management and maintaining a healthy body weight. By regulating the amount of food you consume, you can avoid overeating and ensure that your meals are balanced and nutritious.

Role of Portion Control:

- **Blood Sugar Regulation:** Controlling portion sizes helps prevent large fluctuations in blood sugar levels, which is essential for managing diabetes.

- **Weight Management:** Proper portion control is key to achieving and maintaining a healthy weight, which can improve insulin sensitivity and reduce the risk of diabetes-related complications.
- **Nutrient Balance:** It ensures that you get the right amounts of different nutrients without consuming excess calories.

Practical Techniques for Measuring Portions:

- **Measuring Cups and Spoons:** These are simple tools that can help you measure accurate portions of foods like rice, pasta, and cereal.
- **Kitchen Scale:** A digital scale can provide the most precise measurement for various foods, especially for items like meat and cheese that can be harder to gauge with cups and spoons.
- **Visual Comparisons:** If you don't have measuring tools handy, you can use everyday objects as visual guides for portion sizes. For example, a serving of meat should be about the size of a deck of cards, and a serving of vegetables should be about the size of a baseball.
- **Plate Method:** Another approach is to use your plate as a guide. Fill half of your plate with non-starchy vegetables, one-quarter with lean protein, and one-quarter with whole grains or starchy vegetables.

By incorporating these portion control techniques into your daily routine, you can take an active role in managing your diabetes and promoting your overall health.

MEAL PLANNING TOOLS AND TECHNIQUES

- **Meal Planning Apps:** Numerous apps are available that can help you plan your meals, track your food intake, and monitor your blood sugar levels. These apps often come with features like recipe suggestions, grocery lists, and nutritional information, making it easier to stick to your meal plan.
- **Food Diaries:** Keeping a food diary can be a simple yet powerful tool for managing diabetes. By recording everything you eat and drink, you can gain insights into your eating habits, identify patterns, and make necessary adjustments to your diet.
- **Portion-Divided Plates:** Plates with portion divisions can be a helpful visual guide for controlling portion sizes. They typically have sections for non-starchy vegetables, proteins, and carbohydrates, helping you create balanced meals without having to measure everything.

Weekly Meal Plan Organization:

- **Plan Your Meals:** Start by deciding what you'll eat for breakfast, lunch, dinner, and snacks throughout the week. Consider your schedule, food preferences, and nutritional needs.
- **Make a Grocery List:** Based on your meal plan, create a list of all the ingredients you'll need. This can help you stay focused and avoid impulse buys at the grocery store.
- **Prep in Advance:** Prepare ingredients or entire meals ahead of time. For example, you can chop vegetables, cook grains, or portion out snacks for the week.
- **Be Flexible:** While it's important to have a plan, be prepared to adjust based on your blood sugar levels, cravings, or unexpected events.

By utilizing these tools and techniques, you can make meal planning and portion control more manageable and effective, leading to better diabetes management and overall health.

CREATE BALANCED MEALS

Creating balanced meals is crucial for managing diabetes and maintaining overall health. A balanced meal includes all essential food groups, with an emphasis on nutrients that are particularly important for diabetics. Here's a guide to help you build balanced meals:

Include All Essential Food Groups:

- **Non-Starchy Vegetables:** Fill half of your plate with non-starchy vegetables like leafy greens, bell peppers, broccoli, and zucchini. These are low in carbs and high in fiber, vitamins, and minerals.
- **Lean Proteins:** Allocate one-quarter of your plate to lean protein sources such as chicken, fish, tofu, legumes, or eggs. Protein is essential for tissue repair and can help stabilize blood sugar levels.
- **Healthy Carbohydrates:** The remaining quarter of your plate should consist of healthy carbohydrates, such as whole grains (quinoa, brown rice, whole wheat pasta) or starchy vegetables (sweet potatoes, corn). These provide energy and are rich in fiber, which helps manage blood sugar levels.
- **Healthy Fats:** Incorporate a small amount of healthy fats into your meal, such as olive oil, avocados, or nuts. These facts are important for heart health and can help with satiety.

Examples of Balanced Meals:

Breakfast:

Scrambled eggs with spinach and tomatoes, served with a slice of whole-grain toast and a side of berries.

Lunch:

Grilled chicken salad with mixed greens, cucumbers, bell peppers, and a vinaigrette dressing, accompanied by a small serving of quinoa.

Dinner:

Baked salmon with a side of steamed broccoli and a sweet potato.

Snacks:

- A small apple with a tablespoon of almond butter.
- A handful of mixed nuts and a few slices of cucumber.

When creating balanced meals, it's important to pay attention to portion sizes and the glycemic index of the foods you choose. This will help you maintain stable blood sugar levels and manage your diabetes effectively. Experiment with different combinations of foods to find meals that you enjoy and that fit into your diabetes management plan.

TIPS FOR EATING OUT

Eating out can be challenging when managing diabetes, but with a few strategies, you can enjoy dining at restaurants while staying in control of your portions and making healthy food choices. Here are some tips to help you navigate eating out:

Plan:

- **Research the Menu:** Before you go to the restaurant, check the menu online to identify healthier options. Look for dishes that are grilled, baked, or steamed, and avoid those that are fried or smothered in heavy sauces.
- **Decide What to Order:** Decide what you'll order in advance to avoid making impulsive decisions when you're hungry.

Control Portions:

- **Share Your Meal:** Restaurant portions are often larger than what you would eat at home. Consider sharing a dish with a dining companion or ask for half of your meal to be boxed up before it's served.
- **Start with a Salad:** Order a salad with a light dressing to start your meal. This can help you feel fuller and prevent overeating.

Make Healthy Choices:

- **Choose Lean Proteins:** Opt for dishes that feature lean proteins like grilled chicken, fish, or tofu.
- **Load Up on Vegetables:** Look for meals that include a variety of non-starchy vegetables. If your dish has a small veggie side, ask for extra.
- **Be Mindful of Carbohydrates:** Choose whole-grain options when available and be cautious of dishes with large amounts of pasta, rice, or bread.

Do's and Don'ts on Restaurant Menus:

Do:

- Do choose dishes that are grilled, baked, or steamed.
- Do ask for dressings and sauces on the side so you can control the amount.
- Do opt for water, unsweetened tea, or other non-caloric beverages.

Don't:

- Don't order dishes that are fried, breaded, or come with creamy sauces.
- Don't be afraid to ask for substitutions, such as a side salad instead of fries.
- Don't forget to account for the carbs in alcoholic beverages if you choose to drink.

By following these tips, you can enjoy eating out without compromising your diabetic diet. Remember to listen to your body and stop eating when you're full to avoid overindulging.

TAILOR RECIPES AND PORTIONS TO THE FAMILY

Managing diabetes doesn't mean you have to prepare separate meals for yourself and your family. With a few adjustments, you can create meals that are healthy for everyone and cater to your specific dietary needs. Here are some tips on how to adapt portions and recipes for the whole family:

Modify Recipes:

- **Increase Vegetables:** Boost the nutritional value of meals by adding more non-starchy vegetables. For example, add extra veggies to stir-fries, soups, and casseroles.
- **Use Whole Grains:** Replace white rice, pasta, and bread with whole-grain alternatives like brown rice, whole wheat pasta, and whole grain bread. These are healthier options for everyone and better for blood sugar control.
- **Choose Lean Proteins:** Opt for lean protein sources such as chicken breast, fish, tofu, or legumes. These are good for the whole family and can be cooked in various ways to suit everyone's taste.

Adjust Portions:

- **Serve Family Style:** Instead of plating individual portions, serve meals family-style, allowing everyone to take the amount they need. This makes it easier to control your own portion sizes.
- **Use Smaller Plates:** Using smaller plates for your own meals can help you manage portion sizes without feeling deprived.

Involve the Family:

- **Meal Planning:** Involve your family in planning meals for the week. This can help ensure that the menu includes something for everyone and teaches your family about healthy eating.
- **Food Preparation:** Get your family involved in preparing meals. Assign tasks such as washing vegetables, setting the table, or stirring the pot. This can make mealtime more enjoyable and less of a chore for you.

Educate Your Family:

- **Discuss Nutrition:** Educate your family about the importance of a balanced diet and how it can benefit everyone, not just those with diabetes.
- **Lead by Example:** Show your family that eating healthily can be delicious and satisfying. Your positive attitude towards food can influence their eating habits.

By adapting recipes and portions to meet the needs of your whole family, you can create a supportive environment for managing your diabetes while ensuring everyone enjoys nutritious and delicious meals.

MONITORING AND EVALUATION

In managing diabetes, it's crucial to monitor your progress and evaluate the effectiveness of your dietary choices. Regular monitoring and evaluation can help you stay on track, make necessary adjustments, and achieve your health goals. Here are some key strategies for effective monitoring and evaluation:

Blood Glucose Monitoring:

- **Regular Testing:** Check your blood glucose levels regularly, as advised by your healthcare provider. This can help you understand how different foods and meals affect your blood sugar.
- **Record Keeping:** Keep a log of your blood glucose readings, along with notes on what you ate and any other relevant factors, such as exercise or stress. This can help you identify patterns and make informed adjustments to your diet.

Food Journaling:

- **Track Your Meals:** Use a food journal or an app to record everything you eat and drink. Be sure to note portion sizes and the timing of your meals.
- **Review Your Journal:** Periodically review your food journal to assess your eating habits, identify areas for improvement, and ensure you're meeting your nutritional goals.

Consultation with Healthcare Professionals:

- **Regular Check-ups:** Schedule regular appointments with your healthcare provider or dietitian to review your progress and discuss any challenges you're facing.
- **Adjustments:** Based on your monitoring and evaluation, your healthcare team may suggest changes to your meal plan, medication, or lifestyle to better manage your diabetes.

Setting and Reviewing Goals:

- **Set Realistic Goals:** Establish clear, achievable goals for your diabetes management, such as maintaining stable blood glucose levels, losing weight, or improving your overall diet.
- **Regularly Review Your Goals:** Check in on your goals regularly to assess your progress and make any necessary adjustments.

By consistently monitoring and evaluating your dietary choices and overall diabetes management, you can make informed decisions that lead to better health outcomes. Remember, managing diabetes is an ongoing process, and it's okay to make changes along the way to find what works best for you.

CHAPTER 5: HEALTHY LIFESTYLES FOR DIABETICS

Living with diabetes requires more than just careful meal planning; it also involves adopting a healthy lifestyle that supports your overall well-being. In this chapter, we'll explore the crucial role of physical activity in managing diabetes and provide practical advice for incorporating exercise into your daily routine, regardless of your age or fitness level.

THE IMPORTANCE OF PHYSICAL ACTIVITY

Physical activity is a key component of diabetes management. Regular exercise can help regulate blood glucose levels, improve insulin sensitivity, and maintain a healthy weight. Here's why physical activity is so important for diabetics:

- **Blood Glucose Regulation:** Exercise helps your muscles use glucose more efficiently, which can lower blood sugar levels.
- **Weight Management:** Staying active helps burn calories and can prevent or reduce obesity, a major risk factor for type 2 diabetes.
- **Heart Health:** Regular exercise can help reduce the risk of heart disease, which is higher in individuals with diabetes.
- **Mental Well-being:** Physical activity can also improve mood and reduce stress, which is beneficial for overall mental health.

Examples of Physical Activity for Diabetics:

- **Walking:** A simple and effective way to start. Aim for at least 30 minutes a day, five days a week.
- **Cycling:** A low-impact exercise that's great for cardiovascular health.
- **Swimming:** Provides a full-body workout with minimal stress on joints.
- **Yoga:** Helps improve flexibility, balance, and stress management.
- **Strength Training:** Building muscle can improve insulin sensitivity and glucose metabolism. Use light weights or resistance bands to start.

Tips for Starting and Maintaining an Exercise Routine:

- **Consult Your Doctor:** Before starting any new exercise program, consult your healthcare provider to ensure it's safe for you.
- **Start Slowly:** Begin with low-intensity activities and gradually increase intensity and duration.
- **Find Activities You Enjoy:** You're more likely to stick with exercise if you enjoy it. Try different activities to find what you like.
- **Set Realistic Goals:** Establish achievable goals and celebrate your progress.
- **Monitor Your Blood Sugar:** Keep track of your blood glucose levels before and after exercise to understand how different activities affect you.

STRESS MANAGEMENT

Managing stress is an essential part of diabetes care, as stress can have a significant impact on blood glucose levels and overall well-being. When you're stressed, your body releases hormones that can raise your blood sugar. Therefore, finding effective ways to reduce stress is crucial for maintaining good diabetes control. Here are some stress-reducing techniques and tips for incorporating them into your daily routine:

Yoga: Yoga combines physical postures, breathing exercises, and meditation to promote relaxation and reduce stress. It can also improve flexibility, strength, and balance. Consider joining a yoga class or following online tutorials to get started.

Meditation: Meditation involves focusing your mind to achieve a state of calm. It can help reduce stress, improve emotional well-being, and enhance focus. Try starting with just a few minutes of meditation each day and gradually increase the duration.

Breathing Techniques: Deep breathing exercises can help calm your mind and reduce stress. One simple technique is the 4-7-8 breath: inhale for 4 seconds, hold your breath for 7 seconds, and exhale slowly for 8 seconds. Repeat this cycle for a few minutes to feel more relaxed.

Mindfulness: Mindfulness is the practice of being present and fully engaged in the moment. It can help reduce stress and improve your response to challenging situations. Try incorporating mindfulness into your daily activities, such as eating, walking, or even doing household chores.

Regular Exercise: Physical activity is not only good for your physical health but also your mental health. Regular exercise can help reduce stress, improve mood, and increase energy levels.

Adequate Sleep: Getting enough quality sleep is crucial for stress management. Aim for 7-9 hours of sleep per night and establish a regular sleep routine.

Social Support: Connecting with friends, family, or support groups can provide emotional support and help reduce stress. Don't hesitate to reach out to others when you're feeling overwhelmed.

Time Management: Organize your schedule to avoid last-minute rushes and try to set aside time for relaxation and activities you enjoy.

Seek Professional Help: If stress becomes overwhelming, consider seeking the help of a mental health professional. They can provide coping strategies and support tailored to your needs.

THE ROLE OF SLEEP

Sleep plays a crucial role in diabetes management, as it directly impacts blood glucose levels and overall health. Poor sleep quality or insufficient sleep can disrupt blood sugar control and increase the risk of developing diabetes-related complications. Understanding the link between sleep and diabetes control is essential for maintaining good health.

Link Between Sleep and Diabetes Control:

- **Hormonal Balance:** Sleep helps regulate hormones that control appetite and blood sugar levels. Lack of sleep can lead to hormonal imbalances, which can affect insulin sensitivity and glucose metabolism.
- **Stress Reduction:** Adequate sleep helps reduce stress, which can positively impact blood glucose levels.
- **Weight Management:** Poor sleep is associated with weight gain, a risk factor for type 2 diabetes. Good sleep hygiene supports healthy weight management.

Tips for Improving Sleep Hygiene:

- **Establish a Routine:** Go to bed and wake up at the same time every day, even on weekends, to regulate your body's internal clock.
- **Create a Restful Environment:** Ensure your bedroom is quiet, dark, and cool. Consider using earplugs, eye shades, or white noise machines if needed.
- **Limit Screen Time:** Avoid screens (phones, tablets, computers, TV) at least an hour before bedtime, as the blue light emitted can interfere with your body's natural sleep-wake cycle.
- **Watch Your Diet:** Avoid large meals, caffeine, and alcohol close to bedtime, as they can disrupt sleep.
- **Relax Before Bed:** Develop a relaxing bedtime routine, such as reading a book, taking a warm bath, or practicing relaxation techniques like deep breathing or meditation.

Addressing Common Sleep Problems:

- **Insomnia:** If you have trouble falling asleep or staying asleep, consider practicing relaxation techniques or seeking help from a healthcare professional.
- **Sleep Apnea:** Sleep apnea is common in people with diabetes and can significantly impact sleep quality. If you suspect you have sleep apnea, consult your doctor for a proper diagnosis and treatment.

DAILY HEALTHY HABITS

Developing and maintaining daily healthy habits is essential for effective diabetes management. Small, consistent actions can have a significant impact on your blood sugar levels and overall health. Here are some tips for establishing habits that support your diabetes care:

Adequate Hydration:

- **Drink Water Regularly:** Aim for at least 8-10 cups of water a day to stay hydrated. Water helps regulate blood sugar levels and supports kidney function.
- **Limit Sugary Drinks:** Avoid beverages high in sugar, such as sodas and sweetened juices, as they can cause spikes in blood glucose.

Avoid Smoking:

- **Seek Support:** If you smoke, consider quitting. Smoking can increase the risk of diabetes complications. Talk to your healthcare provider about resources and support for quitting.

Limit Alcohol Intake:

- **Drink in Moderation:** If you choose to drink alcohol, do so in moderation (up to one drink per day for women and up to two drinks per day for men) and always with food to prevent hypoglycemia.
- **Choose Lower-Carb Options:** Opt for drinks with fewer carbohydrates, such as light beer or wine, and avoid sugary cocktails.

Create a Healthy Home Environment:

- **Stock Healthy Foods:** Keep your pantry and fridge stocked with healthy food options, such as fresh fruits and vegetables, whole grains, and lean proteins.
- **Organize Your Space:** Arrange your kitchen and dining area to encourage healthy eating habits. For example, keep fruit on the counter for easy snacking and use smaller plates to control portion sizes.
- **Plan for Physical Activity:** Set up a designated area for exercise at home or keep workout equipment like resistance bands or a yoga mat readily available.

Incorporate Regular Physical Activity:

- **Stay Active:** Aim for at least 150 minutes of moderate-intensity aerobic exercise each week, such as brisk walking, swimming, or cycling.
- **Break Up Sitting Time:** Try to stand up and move around for a few minutes every hour, especially if you have a sedentary job.

PREVENTION OF COMPLICATIONS

Diabetes can lead to various complications if not managed properly. However, with careful monitoring and preventive measures, you can reduce the risk of these complications. Here are some strategies to help you stay on top of your health:

Foot Problems:

- **Daily Foot Inspections:** Check your feet every day for cuts, blisters, redness, or swelling. Use a mirror or ask for help if you can't see the bottoms of your feet.
- **Proper Footwear:** Wear comfortable, well-fitting shoes to protect your feet from injuries. Avoid walking barefoot, even indoors.
- **Regular Foot Care:** Keep your feet clean and dry. Moisturize them to prevent dry skin but avoid applying lotion between your toes.

Eye Health:

- **Regular Eye Exams:** Schedule annual eye exams with an ophthalmologist or optometrist to check for signs of diabetic retinopathy and other eye problems.
- **Control Blood Sugar:** Keeping your blood sugar levels within the target range can help prevent or slow the progression of diabetic eye diseases.

Cardiovascular Health:

- **Blood Pressure and Cholesterol:** Regularly monitor your blood pressure and cholesterol levels. High levels can increase the risk of heart disease and stroke.
- **Healthy Lifestyle:** To protect your cardiovascular health, maintain a heart-healthy diet, engage in regular physical activity, and avoid smoking.

Regular Medical Checkups:

- **Routine Checkups:** Visit your healthcare provider regularly for checkups and screenings. These visits are crucial for detecting any potential complications early.
- **Communication with Healthcare Team:** Keep an open line of communication with your healthcare team. Share any concerns or changes in your health and follow their recommendations for managing your diabetes.

By implementing these strategies and staying vigilant about your health, you can effectively prevent or delay the onset of diabetes-related complications. Regular medical checkups and a proactive approach to your well-being are key to maintaining a healthy life with diabetes.

CHAPTER 6: BREAKFAST

TOFU AND VEGETABLE SCRAMBLE

This Tofu and Vegetable Scramble is a nutritious and flavorful way to start your day. Packed with protein from the tofu and loaded with vitamins from the spinach and tomatoes, it's a wholesome breakfast option that's perfect for those managing diabetes. The turmeric not only adds color and flavor but also provides anti-inflammatory benefits. Enjoy this scramble on its own or pair it with whole-grain toast for a more filling meal.

RECIPE 1	NUTRITIONAL VALUES (PER SERVING)			
Difficulty: Easy	**Calories:** 180	**Sodium:** 200mg	**Protein:** 12g	**Sugars:** 2g
Servings: 1	**Fiber:** 3g	**Carbohydrates:** 6g		**Fat:** 12g
Preparation Time: 10 minutes	**Cooking Time:** 10 minutes		**Total Time:** 20 minutes	

INGREDIENTS	GUIDELINES
<ul><li>100g firm tofu, crumbled</li><li>½ cup spinach, chopped</li><li>¼ cup cherry tomatoes, halved</li><li>¼ teaspoon turmeric</li><li>⅛ teaspoon black pepper</li><li>½ tablespoon olive oil</li><li>Salt to taste</li></ul>	1. Heat the olive oil in a non-stick pan over medium heat. 2. Add the crumbled tofu to the pan and cook for 2-3 minutes, stirring occasionally. 3. Sprinkle the turmeric and black pepper over the tofu and stir to combine. The turmeric will give the tofu a golden color and a mild, earthy flavor. 4. Add the chopped spinach and cherry tomatoes to the pan. Cook for another 5-7 minutes, or until the spinach is wilted and the tomatoes are soft. 5. Season with salt to taste and give everything a final stir. 6. Serve hot, garnished with additional black pepper or fresh herbs if desired.

COCONUT CHIA PUDDING

This Coconut Chia Pudding is a delicious and nutritious breakfast option, perfect for those on a diabetic-friendly diet. The chia seeds are a great source of fiber, omega-3 fatty acids, and protein, while the coconut milk adds a creamy texture and a hint of tropical flavor. Topped with fresh raspberries, this pudding is not only tasty but also packed with antioxidants and vitamins. It's a simple and satisfying way to start your day on a healthy note.

RECIPE 2	NUTRITIONAL VALUES (PER SERVING)			
Difficulty: Easy	**Calories:** 200	**Sodium:** 15mg	**Protein:** 4g	**Sugars:** 4g
Servings: 1	**Fiber:** 8g	**Carbohydrates:** 15g		**Fat:** 14g
Preparation Time: 5 minutes	**Cooking Time:** 0 minutes (needs to chill overnight)		**Total Time:** 5 minutes + chilling time	

INGREDIENTS	GUIDELINES
<ul><li>2 tablespoons chia seeds</li><li>½ cup coconut milk</li><li>1 tablespoon honey or maple syrup (adjust to taste)</li><li>¼ teaspoon vanilla extract</li></ul>**Optional toppings:** Fresh berries, sliced almonds, or coconut flakes	1. In a mixing bowl, combine the chia seeds, coconut milk, and vanilla extract. Stir well to ensure the chia seeds are evenly distributed. 2. Cover the bowl and refrigerate the mixture overnight or for at least 6 hours. The chia seeds will absorb the liquid and swell, creating a pudding-like consistency. 3. Before serving, give the pudding a good stir to break up any clumps. If the pudding is too thick, you can add a little more coconut milk to reach your desired consistency. 4. Divide the pudding into serving bowls and top with raspberries. You can also add a drizzle of honey or maple syrup if you prefer a sweeter taste.

CINNAMON OAT WAFFLES

These Cinnamon Oat Waffles offer a heart-healthy and diabetes-friendly twist on a classic breakfast favorite. Made with rolled oats and almond milk, they're high in fiber and low in added sugars, making them a great option for maintaining stable blood sugar levels. The cinnamon adds a warm, comforting flavor, making these waffles a perfect cozy breakfast for any day of the week.

RECIPE 3	NUTRITIONAL VALUES (PER WAFFLE)			
Difficulty: Easy	**Calories:** 220	**Sodium:** 160mg	**Protein:** 2g	**Sugars:** 1g
Servings: 1	**Fiber:** 6g	**Carbohydrates:** 35g		**Fat:** 5g
Preparation Time: 10 minutes	**Cooking Time:** 5 minutes		**Total Time:** 15 minutes	

INGREDIENTS	GUIDELINES

- ½ cup rolled oats, ground into flour
- ¼ teaspoon cinnamon
- ¼ teaspoon baking powder
- 1 egg
- ¼ cup almond milk
- 1 tablespoon unsweetened applesauce
- ½ tablespoon coconut oil, melted
- ½ teaspoon vanilla extract
- Optional: 1 teaspoon honey or maple syrup for sweetness

1. In a blender, combine the rolled oats, almond milk, egg, ground cinnamon, and salt. Blend until the mixture is smooth and the oats are fully ground, about 1-2 minutes.
2. Preheat your waffle iron according to the manufacturer's instructions. Lightly grease the waffle iron with non-stick cooking spray or a small amount of oil.
3. Pour about ½ cup of the batter onto the center of the preheated waffle iron. Close the lid and cook according to your waffle iron's instructions, typically for about 4-5 minutes, or until the waffle is golden brown and crisp.
4. Carefully remove the waffle from the iron and repeat with the remaining batter.
5. Serve the waffles warm, with your choice of toppings such as fresh fruit, a dollop of Greek yogurt, or a drizzle of sugar-free maple syrup.

CARROT AND WALNUT MUFFINS

These Carrot and Walnut Muffins are a delicious and nutritious option for a diabetic-friendly breakfast or snack. Made with almond flour, they're low in carbs and high in healthy fats and fiber, helping to keep blood sugar levels stable. The carrots add natural sweetness and moisture, while the walnuts provide a satisfying crunch. Enjoy these muffins on their own or with a spread of almond butter for an extra protein boost.

RECIPE 4	NUTRITIONAL VALUES (PER MUFFIN)			
Difficulty: Easy	**Calories:** 190	**Sodium:** 75mg	**Protein:** 6g	**Sugars:** 3g
Servings: 1	**Fiber:** 3g	**Carbohydrates:** 10g		**Fat:** 15g
Preparation Time: 15 minutes	**Cooking Time:** 25 minutes		**Total Time:** 40 minutes	

INGREDIENTS	GUIDELINES

- 1 medium carrot, grated
- ¼ cup whole wheat flour
- 1 tablespoon chopped walnuts
- 1 tablespoon raisins (optional)
- 1 egg
- 1 tablespoon olive oil or melted coconut oil
- 1 tablespoon honey or maple syrup
- ¼ teaspoon vanilla extract
- ¼ teaspoon baking soda
- ¼ teaspoon cinnamon
- Pinch of salt

1. Preheat your oven to 350°F (175°C). Line a muffin tin with paper liners or lightly grease the cups.
2. In a large mixing bowl, combine the almond flour, sweetener, ground cinnamon, baking powder, and salt. Stir until well mixed.
3. In a separate bowl, whisk the eggs until lightly beaten. Add the grated carrots and chopped walnuts to the eggs and mix until combined.
4. Add the wet ingredients to the dry ingredients and stir until just combined. Be careful not to overmix.
5. Divide the batter evenly among the muffin cups, filling each about ¾ full.
6. Bake in the preheated oven for 20-25 minutes, or until a toothpick inserted into the center of a muffin comes out clean.
7. Allow the muffins to cool in the pan for 5 minutes, then transfer them to a wire rack to cool completely.

SPINACH & AVOCADO SMOOTHIE

This Spinach and avocado Smoothie is a powerhouse of nutrients, perfect for a quick and healthy breakfast or snack. The spinach provides a dose of greens without overpowering the taste, while the avocado adds creaminess and healthy fats. The banana brings natural sweetness, and the flaxseed offers a boost of fiber and omega-3 fatty acids. This smoothie is a great way to start your day with a serving of fruits and vegetables, keeping you satisfied and energized.

RECIPE 5	NUTRITIONAL VALUES (PER SERVING, IF SERVING 2)			
Difficulty: Easy	**Calories:** 150	**Sodium:** 95mg	**Protein:** 3g	**Sugars:** 7g
Servings: 1	**Fiber:** 5g	**Carbohydrates:** 16g		**Fat:** 9g
Preparation Time: 5 minutes	**Cooking Time:** 0 minutes		**Total Time:** 5 minutes	

INGREDIENTS	GUIDELINES
<ul><li>½ avocado</li><li>1 cup fresh spinach</li><li>½ banana (optional for sweetness)</li><li>½ cup unsweetened almond milk or water</li><li>1 tablespoon chia seeds</li><li>1 teaspoon lemon juice</li><li>Ice cubes (as needed)</li></ul>	1. In a blender, combine the spinach, avocado, frozen banana, almond milk, and ground flaxseed. 2. Blend on high speed until smooth and creamy. If the smoothie is too thick, add a little more almond milk to reach your desired consistency. 3. Taste the smoothie and adjust sweetness if necessary. You can add a drizzle of honey or a few drops of stevia if you prefer a sweeter smoothie. 4. Pour the smoothie into a glass and enjoy immediately. You can garnish with a few spinach leaves or a slice of avocado if desired.

SWEET POTATO CROUTONS

These Sweet Potato Croutons offer a delightful twist on traditional croutons, adding a sweet and savory element to salads or as a standalone snack. The natural sweetness of the sweet potatoes' pairs beautifully with the creamy ricotta, crunchy walnuts, and a hint of cinnamon. Drizzling with honey adds an extra touch of sweetness, making these croutons a versatile and delicious addition to your diabetic-friendly recipe collection.

RECIPE 6	NUTRITIONAL VALUES (PER SERVING)			
Difficulty: Easy	**Calories:** 210	**Sodium:** 100mg	**Protein:** 5g	**Sugars:** 4g (without honey)
Servings: 1	**Fiber:** 3g	**Carbohydrates:** 18g		**Fat:** 14g
Preparation Time: 10 minutes	**Cooking Time:** 25 minutes		**Total Time:** 35 minutes	

INGREDIENTS	GUIDELINES
<ul><li>1 small, sweet potato, peeled and diced into small cubes</li><li>1 tablespoon olive oil</li><li>¼ teaspoon paprika</li><li>¼ teaspoon garlic powder</li><li>Salt and pepper to taste</li></ul>	1. Preheat your oven to 400°F (200°C). Line a baking sheet with parchment paper. 2. In a mixing bowl, toss the diced sweet potatoes with olive oil, cinnamon, and a pinch of salt until evenly coated. 3. Spread the sweet potato cubes in a single layer on the prepared baking sheet. Bake for 25-30 minutes, or until the sweet potatoes are golden and crispy, stirring halfway through for even cooking. 4. While the sweet potatoes are baking, mix the ricotta cheese with a little cinnamon and a pinch of salt in a small bowl. Set aside. 5. Once the sweet potato croutons are done, let them cool for a few minutes. 6. To serve, place a dollop of the seasoned ricotta on each sweet potato cube, sprinkle with chopped walnuts, and drizzle with honey if desired.

MUSHROOM AND THYME OMELETTE

This Mushroom and Thyme Omelette is a savory and aromatic breakfast option that's perfect for anyone managing diabetes. The combination of earthy mushrooms, fresh thyme, and fluffy eggs creates a delicious and satisfying meal that's low in carbs and high in protein. It's a quick and easy recipe that can be enjoyed any time of day, whether for breakfast, brunch, or a light dinner.

RECIPE 7	NUTRITIONAL VALUES (PER SERVING)			
Difficulty: Easy	**Calories:** 310	**Sodium:** 240mg	**Protein:** 21g	**Sugars:** 2g
Servings: 1	**Fiber:** 1g	**Carbohydrates:** 4g		**Fat:** 23g
Preparation Time: 5 minutes	**Cooking Time:** 10 minutes		**Total Time:** 15 minutes	

INGREDIENTS	GUIDELINES
<ul><li>2 eggs</li><li>¼ cup sliced mushrooms</li><li>1 teaspoon fresh thyme leaves</li><li>1 tablespoon grated cheese (optional, choose a low-fat variety for a healthier option)</li><li>1 tablespoon olive oil</li><li>Salt and pepper to taste</li></ul>	1. Whisk the eggs with a pinch of salt in a bowl until well beaten. Set aside. 2. Heat the olive oil in a non-stick skillet over medium heat. Add the sliced mushrooms, and minced garlic, and sauté for about 5 minutes, or until the mushrooms are tender and golden. 3. Sprinkle the fresh thyme leaves over the mushrooms and stir to combine. 4. Pour the beaten eggs over the mushroom and thyme mixture in the skillet. Tilt the pan to ensure the eggs cover the mushrooms evenly. 5. Let the omelette cook for about 2-3 minutes, or until the edges start to set. Using a spatula, gently lift the edges and tilt the pan to allow the uncooked eggs to flow underneath. 6. Once the omelette is set but still slightly runny on top, use the spatula to fold it in half. Let it cook for another minute or two until fully set. 7. Slide the omelette onto a plate and serve immediately.

SPELT AND PEAR PORRIDGE

This Spelt and Pear Porridge is a wholesome and comforting breakfast option that's perfect for a cold morning. Spelt grains provide a nutty flavor and hearty texture, while the pear adds natural sweetness, and the walnuts offer a satisfying crunch. The cinnamon brings a warm and inviting aroma, making this porridge a delightful way to start your day. It's a nutritious meal that's high in fiber and packed with flavor.

RECIPE 8	NUTRITIONAL VALUES (PER SERVING)			
Difficulty: Easy	**Calories:** 350	**Sodium:** 30mg	**Protein:** 8g	**Sugars:** 12g
Servings: 1	**Fiber:** 10g	**Carbohydrates:** 58g		**Fat:** 10g
Preparation Time: 5 minutes	**Cooking Time:** 15 minutes		**Total Time:** 20 minutes	

INGREDIENTS	GUIDELINES
<ul><li>¼ cup spelt grains</li><li>1 small pear, diced</li><li>1 cup water or milk of choice</li><li>1 tablespoon chopped nuts (such as walnuts or almonds)</li><li>1 teaspoon honey or maple syrup (optional)</li><li>¼ teaspoon cinnamon</li></ul>	1. Rinse the spelt grains under cold water and drain. 2. In a medium saucepan, combine the spelt grains and rice milk. Bring to a boil over medium-high heat. 3. Reduce the heat to low, cover, and simmer for about 15-20 minutes, or until the spelt grains are tender and most of the liquid has been absorbed. Stir occasionally to prevent sticking. 4. While the spelt is cooking, prepare the pear by dicing it into small pieces. 5. Once the spelt is cooked, remove the saucepan from the heat. Stir in the diced pear, chopped walnuts, and ground cinnamon. Add a sweetener of your choice if desired. 6. Divide the porridge between two bowls and serve warm. You can garnish with additional walnuts or a sprinkle of cinnamon if you like.

HOMEMADE ENERGY BARS

These Homemade Energy Bars are a delicious and nutritious snack that's perfect for a quick energy boost. Made with natural ingredients like dates, almonds, and quinoa flakes, these bars are packed with fiber, protein, and healthy fats. The pumpkin seeds and chopped coconut add texture and flavor, making these bars a satisfying and convenient option for on-the-go snacking. Enjoy them before or after a workout, or whenever you need a healthy pick-me-up.

RECIPE 9	NUTRITIONAL VALUES (PER BAR, BASED ON 10 SERVINGS)			
Difficulty: Easy	**Calories:** 180	**Sodium:** 5mg	**Protein:** 5g	**Sugars:** 12g
Servings: 1	**Fiber:** 4g	**Carbohydrates:** 22g		**Fat:** 9g
Preparation Time: 10 minutes	**Cooking Time:** 0 minutes (requires chilling)		**Total Time:** 10 minutes + chilling time	

INGREDIENTS	GUIDELINES

INGREDIENTS

- ¼ cup rolled oats
- 1 tablespoon peanut butter or almond butter
- 1 tablespoon honey or maple syrup
- 1 tablespoon dried cranberries or raisins
- 1 tablespoon chopped nuts (such as almonds or walnuts)
- 1 tablespoon seeds (such as pumpkin seeds or sunflower seeds)
- A pinch of salt

GUIDELINES

1. Place the pitted dates in a bowl of warm water for about 10 minutes to soften. Drain the dates and pat them dry with a paper towel.
2. In a food processor, combine the softened dates, raw almonds, quinoa flakes, pumpkin seeds, chopped coconut, and a pinch of salt if desired. Pulse until the mixture is well combined and sticks together when pressed between your fingers. If the mixture is too dry, you can add a tablespoon of water to help it bind.
3. Line a baking dish or tray with parchment paper. Transfer the mixture to the lined dish and press it down firmly into an even layer, about ½ inch thick.
4. Place the dish in the refrigerator and chill for 1-2 hours, or until the mixture is firm.
5. Once chilled, use a sharp knife to cut the mixture into bars or squares. Store the energy bars in an airtight container in the refrigerator for up to a week.

WHOLE WHEAT BLUEBERRY PANCAKES

These Whole Wheat Blueberry Pancakes are a delightful and nutritious breakfast option. Made with whole wheat flour, they're high in fiber and have a hearty texture. The blueberries add a burst of sweetness and are packed with antioxidants. These pancakes are perfect for a weekend brunch or a special breakfast treat. Enjoy them with a cup of coffee or tea for a complete and satisfying meal.

RECIPE 10	NUTRITIONAL VALUES (PER SERVING)			
Difficulty: Easy	**Calories:** 210	**Sodium:** 310mg	**Protein:** 8g	**Sugars:** 6g
Servings: 1	**Fiber:** 6g	**Carbohydrates:** 40g		**Fat:** 3g
Preparation Time: 5 minutes	**Cooking Time:** 10 minutes		**Total Time:** 15 minutes	

INGREDIENTS	GUIDELINES

INGREDIENTS

- ⅓ cup whole wheat flour
- ¼ teaspoon baking powder
- 1 egg
- ¼ cup milk or almond milk
- 1 tablespoon honey or maple syrup (optional)
- ¼ cup fresh blueberries
- 1 tablespoon unsalted butter or coconut oil, for cooking

GUIDELINES

1. Whisk together the whole wheat flour, baking powder, and salt in a large mixing bowl.
2. In a separate bowl, beat the egg and then stir in the goat milk until well combined.
3. Pour the wet ingredients into the dry ingredients and stir gently until just combined. Be careful not to overmix. The batter should be slightly lumpy.
4. Gently fold in the blueberries, being careful not to crush them.
5. Heat a non-stick skillet or griddle over medium heat. Lightly grease it with non-stick cooking spray or a small amount of oil.
6. For each pancake, pour about ¼ cup of batter onto the skillet. Cook for 2-3 minutes, or until bubbles form on the surface and the edges look set. Flip the pancake and cook for an additional 1-2 minutes, or until golden brown and cooked through.
7. Repeat with the remaining batter, greasing the skillet as needed.
8. Serve the pancakes warm with your choice of toppings, such as fresher blueberries, a drizzle of maple syrup, or a dollop of Greek yogurt.

CHAPTER 7: LUNCH

LENTIL AND VEGETABLE SOUP

This Lentil and Vegetable Soup is a hearty and nutritious meal, perfect for a diabetic-friendly lunch. Lentils are an excellent source of protein and fiber, making them great for blood sugar management. The combination of vegetables adds flavor and additional nutrients, while the olive oil provides healthy fats. This soup is comforting, flavorful, and easy to make, making it an ideal choice for a satisfying and healthy lunch.

RECIPE 1	NUTRITIONAL VALUES (PER SERVING)			
Difficulty: Easy	**Calories:** 280	**Sodium:** 300mg	**Protein:** 14g	**Sugars:** 6g
Servings: 1	**Fiber:** 16g	**Carbohydrates:** 40g		**Fat:** 8g
Preparation Time: 10 minutes	**Cooking Time:** 30 minutes		**Total Time:** 40 minutes	

INGREDIENTS	GUIDELINES
<ul><li>¼ cup dried lentils, rinsed</li><li>1 cup vegetable broth or water</li><li>¼ cup diced carrots</li><li>¼ cup diced celery</li><li>¼ cup chopped onion</li><li>1 garlic clove, minced</li><li>½ tablespoon olive oil</li><li>¼ teaspoon dried thyme</li><li>Salt and pepper to taste</li></ul>	1. In a large pot, heat the olive oil over medium heat. Add the onion and garlic, and sauté for 2-3 minutes until the onion is translucent. 2. Add the diced carrots and celery to the pot, and cook for another 5 minutes, stirring occasionally. 3. Stir in the rinsed lentils, diced peeled tomatoes, dried thyme, and vegetable broth. Bring the mixture to a boil. 4. Reduce the heat to low, cover, and simmer for about 35-40 minutes, or until the lentils are tender. 5. Season the soup with salt and pepper to taste. If the soup is too thick, you can add more vegetable broth or water to reach your desired consistency. 6. Serve the soup hot, garnished with fresh parsley if desired.

WHOLE WHEAT SANDWICHES WITH SMOKED SALMON

These Whole Wheat Sandwiches with Smoked Salmon are a delicious and nutritious option for a quick and easy lunch. The whole wheat bread provides a good source of fiber, while the smoked salmon offers high-quality protein and omega-3 fatty acids. The avocado adds creamy texture and healthy fats, and the arugula brings a peppery flavor and extra nutrients. This sandwich is a well-balanced meal that's perfect for anyone looking for a heart-healthy and diabetic-friendly lunch option.

RECIPE 2	NUTRITIONAL VALUES (PER SERVING)			
Difficulty: Easy	**Calories:** 320	**Sodium:** 640mg	**Protein:** 20g	**Sugars:** 5g
Servings: 1	**Fiber:** 8g	**Carbohydrates:** 35g		**Fat:** 12g
Preparation Time: 5 minutes	**Cooking Time:** 0 minutes		**Total Time:** 5 minutes	

INGREDIENTS	GUIDELINES
<ul><li>2 slices of whole wheat bread</li><li>2 ounces smoked salmon</li><li>1 tablespoon cream cheese (choose a low-fat variety for a healthier)</li><li>1 tablespoon red onion, thinly sliced</li><li>A few capers (optional)</li><li>Fresh dill, for garnish</li></ul>	1. Spread a thin layer of mustard on one side of each slice of whole wheat bread. 1. On two of the slices, layer the smoked salmon, avocado slices, and arugula. Sprinkle with freshly ground black pepper to taste. 2. Top each with another slice of bread, mustard side down, to make two sandwiches. 3. Cut the sandwiches in half and serve immediately.

WHOLE WHEAT PASTA PRIMAVERA

This Whole Wheat Pasta Primavera is a light and flavorful dish that's perfect for a diabetic-friendly lunch. The whole wheat pasta provides a good source of fiber, which is important for blood sugar management. The combination of asparagus, peas, and zucchini adds a variety of nutrients and textures, while the lemon and basil bring a fresh and vibrant flavor to the dish. It's a healthy and satisfying meal that's easy to prepare and sure to please the whole family.

RECIPE 3	NUTRITIONAL VALUES (PER SERVING)			
Difficulty: Easy	**Calories:** 320	**Sodium:** 30mg	**Protein:** 10g	**Sugars:** 5g
Servings: 1	**Fiber:** 10g	**Carbohydrates:** 56g		**Fat:** 8g
Preparation Time: 10 minutes	**Cooking Time:** 15 minutes		**Total Time:** 25 minutes	

INGREDIENTS	GUIDELINES
<ul><li>1 cup whole wheat pasta (such as spaghetti or penne)</li><li>½ cup mixed vegetables (such as bell peppers, broccoli, and carrots), chopped</li><li>1 garlic clove, minced</li><li>1 tablespoon olive oil</li><li>2 tablespoons grated Parmesan cheese (optional)</li><li>Salt and pepper to taste</li><li>Fresh herbs (such as basil or parsley), for garnish</li></ul>	1. Cook the whole wheat pasta according to the package instructions in a large pot of salted boiling water. Drain and set aside. 2. In the same pot, heat the olive oil over medium heat. Add the asparagus and zucchini, and sauté for about 5 minutes, or until they start to soften. 3. Add the peas to the pot and cook for an additional 2-3 minutes, or until the peas are heated through. 4. Return the cooked pasta to the pot with the vegetables. Add the lemon zest, lemon juice, and fresh basil. Toss everything together until well combined. Season with salt and pepper to taste. 5. Serve the pasta primavera warm, garnished with grated Parmesan cheese if desired.

GRILLED CHICKEN WITH YOGURT SAUCE

This Grilled Chicken with Yogurt Sauce is a light and healthy meal that's perfect for a diabetic-friendly lunch or dinner. The chicken is marinated in Greek yogurt and garlic for added flavor and tenderness, then grilled to perfection. The yogurt sauce, with its refreshing combination of cucumber and mint, complements the chicken beautifully. It's a simple yet delicious dish that's high in protein and low in carbs, making it an excellent choice for those managing diabetes.

RECIPE 4	NUTRITIONAL VALUES (PER SERVING)			
Difficulty: Easy	**Calories:** 220	**Sodium:** 150mg	**Protein:** 35g	**Sugars:** 3g
Servings: 1	**Fiber:** 0g	**Carbohydrates:** 6g		**Fat:** 6g
Preparation Time: 10 minutes (plus marinating time)	**Cooking Time:** 10 minutes		**Total Time:** 20 minutes (excluding marinating time)	

INGREDIENTS	GUIDELINES
<ul><li>1 chicken breast (about 6 ounces)</li><li>1/2 cup plain Greek yogurt</li><li>1 garlic clove, minced</li><li>1 tablespoon lemon juice</li><li>1/2 teaspoon dried oregano</li><li>Salt and pepper to taste</li><li>1 tablespoon olive oil (for grilling)</li><li>Fresh herbs (such as parsley or dill), for garnish</li></ul>	6. In a small bowl, mix half of the Greek yogurt, one minced garlic clove, and a pinch of salt. Use this mixture to marinate the chicken breasts. Cover and refrigerate for at least 30 minutes, or up to 2 hours. 7. Preheat your grill to medium-high heat. Brush the grill grates with olive oil to prevent sticking. 8. Remove the chicken from the marinade and season with salt and pepper. Grill the chicken for about 7-8 minutes on each side, or until fully cooked and the internal temperature reaches 165°F (74°C). 9. While the chicken is grilling, prepare the yogurt sauce. In a bowl, combine the remaining Greek yogurt, the other minced garlic clove, diced cucumber, and chopped mint. Season with salt to taste. 10. Once the chicken is cooked, let it rest for a few minutes before slicing. 11. Serve the grilled chicken with a dollop of the yogurt sauce on top.

BROWN RICE WITH SHRIMP AND BROCCOLI

This Brown Rice with Shrimp and Broccoli is a healthy and flavorful dish that's perfect for a diabetic-friendly lunch or dinner. The brown rice provides a good source of whole grains and fiber, while the shrimp is a lean protein option. The broccoli adds a boost of vitamins and minerals, making this meal a nutritious and satisfying choice. The low sodium soy sauce adds a savory depth of flavor without adding too much salt.

RECIPE 5	NUTRITIONAL VALUES (PER SERVING)			
Difficulty: Easy	**Calories:** 340	**Sodium:** 410mg	**Protein:** 26g	**Sugars:** 2g
Servings: 1	**Fiber:** 3g	**Carbohydrates:** 40g		**Fat:** 8g
Preparation Time: 5 minutes	**Cooking Time:** 20 minutes		**Total Time:** 25 minutes	

INGREDIENTS	GUIDELINES
<ul><li>½ cup brown rice</li><li>½ cup broccoli florets</li><li>5-6 large shrimp, peeled and deveined</li><li>1 garlic clove, minced</li><li>1 tablespoon soy sauce (low sodium)</li><li>1 teaspoon sesame oil</li><li>½ teaspoon ginger, grated</li><li>1 tablespoon olive oil</li></ul>	1. Cook the brown rice according to package instructions. 2. In a large skillet, heat the olive oil over medium heat. Add the minced garlic and sauté for about 1 minute until fragrant. 3. Add the shrimp to the skillet and cook for 2-3 minutes on each side, or until they turn pink and opaque. Remove the shrimp from the skillet and set aside. 4. In the same skillet, add the broccoli florets and a splash of water. Cover and cook for about 4-5 minutes, or until the broccoli is tender but still crisp. 5. Return the shrimp to the skillet with the broccoli. Add the soy sauce and stir to combine. Cook for an additional 1-2 minutes to heat everything through. 6. Serve the shrimp and broccoli over the cooked brown rice. Season with salt and pepper to taste.

BAKED VEGETABLE PIE

This Baked Vegetable Pie is a delicious and nutritious way to enjoy a variety of vegetables in one dish. The sweet potatoes, zucchini, and peppers provide a colorful and flavorful base, while the eggs and cheese add protein and calcium. The fresh herbs bring a burst of flavor and aroma to the pie. It's a versatile recipe that can be adapted to include your favorite vegetables and herbs. Serve it as a main dish for lunch or dinner, paired with a side salad for a complete meal.

RECIPE 6	NUTRITIONAL VALUES (PER SERVING)			
Difficulty: Moderate	**Calories:** 220	**Sodium:** 300mg	**Protein:** 12g	**Sugars:** 8g
Servings: 1	**Fiber:** 4g	**Carbohydrates:** 20g		**Fat:** 10g
Preparation Time: 15 minutes	**Cooking Time:** 30 minutes		**Total Time:** 45 minutes	

INGREDIENTS	GUIDELINES
<ul><li>1 small whole wheat pie crust (or homemade with whole wheat flour)</li><li>½ cup mixed vegetables (such as carrots, peas, and corn)</li><li>¼ onion, chopped</li><li>1 garlic clove, minced</li><li>½ cup spinach, chopped</li><li>¼ cup ricotta cheese or a dairy-free alternative</li><li>1 egg</li><li>1 tablespoon olive oil</li><li>Salt and pepper to taste</li><li>1 teaspoon herbs (e.g. thyme, rosemary)</li></ul>	1. Preheat the oven to 375°F (190°C). Lightly grease a 9-inch pie dish with olive oil. 2. Arrange a layer of sweet potato slices at the bottom of the pie dish, overlapping slightly. Season with salt and pepper. 3. Add a layer of zucchini slices on top of the sweet potatoes, followed by a layer of bell pepper slices. Sprinkle with some of the chopped herbs. 4. Repeat the layers until all the vegetables are used, seasoning each layer with salt and pepper. 5. In a mixing bowl, whisk the eggs and pour them evenly over the layered vegetables. Make sure the eggs seep into the layers. 6. Sprinkle the grated cheese on top and finish with a sprinkle of the remaining herbs. 7. Bake in the preheated oven for 40 minutes, or until the eggs are set and the cheese is golden brown. 8. Let the vegetable pie cool for a few minutes before slicing and serving.

VEGETARIAN SANDWICH WITH HUMMUS

This Vegetarian Sandwich with Hummus is a light and refreshing option for a diabetic-friendly lunch. The whole wheat bread provides a good source of fiber, while the hummus adds protein and healthy fats. The fresh vegetables offer a variety of vitamins and minerals, as well as a satisfying crunch. It's a simple and nutritious sandwich that's perfect for a quick and easy meal. Enjoy it with a side of fresh fruit or a handful of nuts for a balanced and satisfying lunch.

RECIPE 7	NUTRITIONAL VALUES (PER SERVING)			
Difficulty: Easy	**Calories:** 280	**Sodium:** 460mg	**Protein:** 12g	**Sugars:** 8g
Servings: 1	**Fiber:** 10g	**Carbohydrates:** 44g		**Fat:** 8g
Preparation Time: 5 minutes	**Cooking Time:** 0 minutes		**Total Time:** 5 minutes	

INGREDIENTS	GUIDELINES
<ul><li>2 slices of whole wheat bread</li><li>2 tablespoons hummus</li><li>¼ cucumber, sliced</li><li>¼ bell pepper, sliced</li><li>A few slices of tomato</li><li>A few leaves of lettuce</li><li>**Optional:** Sprouts or avocado slices for extra nutrition and flavor</li></ul>	1. Spread a generous layer of hummus on one side of each slice of whole wheat bread. 2. On two of the slices, layer the tomato, cucumber, radishes, and lettuce leaves. Season with salt and pepper to taste. 3. Top each with another slice of bread, hummus side down, to make two sandwiches. 4. Cut the sandwiches in half and serve immediately.

CHICKPEA AND TUNA SALAD

This Chickpea and Tuna Salad is a hearty and nutritious dish that's perfect for a diabetic-friendly lunch. The chickpeas provide a good source of fiber and protein, while the tuna adds lean protein and omega-3 fatty acids. The fresh lemon juice and olive oil dressing adds a bright and zesty flavor to the salad. It's a simple and satisfying meal that's easy to prepare and packed with nutrients. Enjoy it on its own or serve it over a bed of greens for a complete and balanced meal.

RECIPE 8	NUTRITIONAL VALUES (PER SERVING)			
Difficulty: Easy	**Calories:** 240	**Sodium:** 320mg	**Protein:** 18g	**Sugars:** 4g
Servings: 1	**Fiber:** 6g	**Carbohydrates:** 23g		**Fat:** 9g
Preparation Time: 10 minutes	**Cooking Time:** 0 minutes		**Total Time:** 10 minutes	

INGREDIENTS	GUIDELINES
<ul><li>½ cup chickpeas, drained and rinsed</li><li>3 ounces canned tuna, drained</li><li>¼ red onion, finely chopped</li><li>¼ bell pepper, diced</li><li>A handful of cherry tomatoes, halved</li><li>1 tablespoon olive oil</li><li>1 tablespoon lemon juice</li><li>Salt and pepper to taste</li><li>Fresh herbs (such as parsley or basil), chopped</li></ul>	1. In a large mixing bowl, combine the chickpeas, flaked tuna, chopped red onion, and chopped parsley. 2. In a small bowl, whisk together the lemon juice and olive oil. Season with salt and pepper to taste. 3. Pour the lemon-olive oil dressing over the chickpea and tuna mixture. Toss gently to coat all the ingredients evenly. 4. Taste and adjust the seasoning if necessary. Let the salad sit for a few minutes to allow the flavors to meld. 5. Serve the salad chilled or at room temperature.

VEGETABLE & COCONUT CURRY

This Vegetable & Coconut Curry is a delicious and creamy dish that's perfect for a diabetic-friendly lunch or dinner. The combination of broccoli and carrots provides a good source of vitamins and fiber, while the coconut milk adds a rich and creamy texture. The curry powder and coriander bring a wonderful depth of flavor to the dish. It's a comforting and satisfying meal that's easy to prepare and full of nutrients.

RECIPE 9	NUTRITIONAL VALUES (PER SERVING)			
Difficulty: Easy	**Calories:** 250	**Sodium:** 55mg	**Protein:** 4g	**Sugars:** 6g
Servings: 1	**Fiber:** 4g	**Carbohydrates:** 14g		**Fat:** 21g
Preparation Time: 10 minutes	**Cooking Time:** 20 minutes		**Total Time:** 30 minutes	

INGREDIENTS	GUIDELINES

- ½ cup mixed vegetables (such as bell peppers, carrots, and peas)
- ¼ cup coconut milk
- ¼ onion, chopped
- 1 garlic clove, minced
- ½ tablespoon curry powder
- ½ teaspoon turmeric
- 1 teaspoon coconut oil
- Salt and pepper to taste
- Fresh cilantro for garnish

1. Heat the olive oil in a large skillet or wok over medium heat. Add the chopped onion and sauté for about 5 minutes, or until softened.
2. Stir in the curry powder and cook for an additional 1-2 minutes to release the flavors.
3. Pour in the coconut milk and bring the mixture to a simmer.
4. Add the broccoli and carrots to the skillet. Cover and cook for about 10-12 minutes, or until the vegetables are tender but still slightly crisp.
5. Season the curry with salt to taste. If you prefer a thinner curry, you can add a little water to adjust the consistency.
6. Just before serving, stir in the chopped coriander for a fresh burst of flavor.
7. Serve the vegetable and coconut curry over cooked brown rice or quinoa for a complete meal.

MINESTRONE RICH IN PROTEIN

This Minestrone Rich in Protein is a hearty and nutritious soup that's perfect for a diabetic-friendly meal. The borlotti beans and lentils provide a good source of protein and fiber, making this soup filling and satisfying. The variety of vegetables adds vitamins and minerals, while the oregano and garlic bring a lovely flavor to the dish. It's a warming and comforting meal that's ideal for a cozy lunch or dinner.

RECIPE 10	NUTRITIONAL VALUES (PER SERVING)			
Difficulty: Easy	**Calories:** 250	**Sodium:** 200mg	**Protein:** 14g	**Sugars:** 8g
Servings: 1	**Fiber:** 12g	**Carbohydrates:** 40g		**Fat:** 5g
Preparation Time: 10 minutes	**Cooking Time:** 25 minutes		**Total Time:** 35 minutes	

INGREDIENTS	GUIDELINES

- ¼ cup canned kidney beans, drained and rinsed & ¼ cup canned chickpeas, drained and rinsed
- ½ cup chopped tomatoes
- ¼ onion, chopped
- 1 garlic clove, minced
- ½ carrot, diced, ½ celery stalk, diced
- ½ zucchini, diced, ½ cup spinach leaves
- 2 cups vegetable broth
- 1 tablespoon olive oil
- ¼ teaspoon dried basil
- ¼ teaspoon dried oregano
- Salt and pepper to taste
- Grated Parmesan cheese for garnish (optional)

1. Heat the olive oil in a large pot over medium heat. Add the chopped onion and minced garlic, and sauté for about 5 minutes until the onion is translucent.
2. Add the diced carrots and sauté for another 3 minutes.
3. Stir in the dried lentils, borlotti beans, diced tomatoes, dried oregano, and vegetable broth. Bring the mixture to a boil.
4. Reduce the heat to low, cover, and simmer for about 20 minutes.
5. Add the diced zucchinis and chopped cabbage to the pot. Continue to simmer for another 10-15 minutes, or until the lentils and vegetables are tender.
6. Season the soup with salt and pepper to taste. If the soup is too thick, you can add more vegetable broth or water to reach your desired consistency.
7. Serve the minestrone hot, garnished with fresh parsley if desired.

GRILLED FISH TACOS

These Grilled Fish Tacos are a light and flavorful option for a diabetic-friendly lunch or dinner. The white fish provides a lean source of protein, while the avocado adds healthy fats. The red cabbage and lime bring a crunchy texture and a zesty flavor to the tacos. Served on corn tortillas, these tacos are a delicious and nutritious meal that's easy to prepare and perfect for a quick weeknight dinner or a casual get-together.

RECIPE 11	NUTRITIONAL VALUES (PER SERVING, 2 TACOS)			
Difficulty: Easy	**Calories:** 320	**Sodium:** 150mg	**Protein:** 25g	**Sugars:** 3g
Servings: 1	**Fiber:** 6g	**Carbohydrates:** 32g		**Fat:** 12g
Preparation Time: 15 minutes	**Cooking Time:** 10 minutes		**Total Time:** 25 minutes	

INGREDIENTS	GUIDELINES

- 1 small fillet of white fish (such as tilapia or cod), about 4-6 ounces
- 2 small corn tortillas
- ¼ cup shredded cabbage
- ¼ avocado, sliced
- 1 tablespoon fresh cilantro, chopped
- 1 lime wedge
- 1 tablespoon plain yogurt or sour cream
- 1 teaspoon taco seasoning
- 1 tablespoon olive oil

1. Preheat your grill to medium-high heat. Brush the fish fillets with olive oil and season with salt and pepper.
2. Grill the fish for 4-5 minutes on each side, or until it flakes easily with a fork. Remove from the grill and let it rest for a few minutes. Then, flake the fish into bite-sized pieces using a fork.
3. While the fish is grilling, warm the corn tortillas on the grill for about 30 seconds on each side, or until they are slightly charred and pliable.
4. To assemble the tacos, divide the flaked fish evenly among the warm tortillas. Top each taco with sliced avocado and red cabbage.
5. Squeeze fresh lime juice over the tacos and garnish with fresh cilantro if desired.
6. Serve the fish tacos immediately, with extra lime wedges on the side for additional flavor.

BROWN RICE AND SALMON BOWL

This Brown Rice and Salmon Bowl is a nutritious and satisfying meal that's perfect for a diabetic-friendly lunch or dinner. The combination of brown rice, salmon, and edamame provides a balanced mix of carbohydrates, protein, and healthy fats. The avocado adds creaminess and additional healthy fats, while the sesame seeds offer a nutty flavor and a crunchy texture. It's a wholesome and delicious bowl that's easy to prepare and full of nutrients.

RECIPE 12	NUTRITIONAL VALUES (PER SERVING)			
Difficulty: Easy	**Calories:** 450	**Sodium:** 200mg	**Protein:** 30g	**Sugars:** 2g
Servings: 1	**Fiber:** 6g	**Carbohydrates:** 38g		**Fat:** 20g
Preparation Time: 5 minutes	**Cooking Time:** 20 minutes		**Total Time:** 25 minutes	

INGREDIENTS	GUIDELINES

- 1 salmon fillet (about 4-6 ounces)
- ½ cup cooked brown rice
- ½ cup broccoli florets
- ¼ avocado, sliced
- 1 tablespoon soy sauce (low sodium)
- 1 teaspoon sesame seeds
- 1 teaspoon olive oil
- Optional garnishes: sliced green onions, a wedge of lemon

1. Preheat your oven to 400°F (200°C). Line a baking sheet with parchment paper.
2. Place the salmon fillets on the prepared baking sheet. Brush them with olive oil and season with salt and pepper.
3. Bake the salmon in the preheated oven for 12-15 minutes, or until it is cooked through and flakes easily with a fork.
4. While the salmon is baking, prepare the brown rice according to package instructions, if not already cooked.
5. In a dry skillet over medium heat, toast the sesame seeds for 2-3 minutes, or until they are golden and fragrant. Stir frequently to prevent burning.
6. To assemble the bowls, divide the cooked brown rice among four bowls. Top each bowl with a baked salmon fillet, sliced avocado, and cooked edamame.
7. Sprinkle the toasted sesame seeds over each bowl. If desired, drizzle soy sauce or teriyaki sauce over the top for added flavor.
8. Serve the bowls immediately, while the salmon is warm.

BAKED COD WITH TOMATO AND OLIVE SAUCE

This Baked Cod with Tomato and Olive Sauce recipe is an ideal dinner option for those managing diabetes. It combines the mild, flaky texture of cod with a robust sauce of cherry tomatoes and black olives, enriching the dish without overwhelming it. Paired with steamed vegetables, this meal is low in carbohydrates and rich in essential nutrients, providing a balanced and satisfying dinner. It's also quick to prepare, making it perfect for a healthy weeknight meal.

RECIPE 13	NUTRITIONAL VALUES (PER SERVING)			
Difficulty: Easy	**Calories:** 320	**Sodium:** 380mg	**Protein:** 28g	**Sugars:** 10g
Servings: 1	**Fiber:** 6g	**Carbohydrates:** 20g		**Fat:** 14g
Preparation Time: 10 minutes	**Cooking Time:** 20 minutes		**Total Time:** 30 minutes	

INGREDIENTS	GUIDELINES
<ul><li>1 (200 g) cod fillet</li><li>1 cup cherry tomatoes, halved</li><li>1/4 cup black olives, pitted and chopped</li><li>2 cloves garlic, minced</li><li>1 teaspoon dried oregano</li><li>1 teaspoon extra virgin olive oil</li><li>Salt and black pepper to taste</li><li>1 cup steamed broccoli</li><li>1 cup steamed carrots</li></ul>	1. Preheat the oven to 200°C (400°F). 2. Place the cod fillet in a lightly oiled baking dish, season the fillet with salt and pepper. 3. In a bowl, combine the halved cherry tomatoes, chopped black olives, minced garlic, and oregano, drizzle the mixture with olive oil and stir to mix, Spread the tomato and olive sauce over the cod in the baking dish. 4. Bake in the preheated oven for about 15-20 minutes, or until the fish is cooked through and flakes easily with a fork. 5. While the fish is baking, steam the broccoli and carrots until they are tender yet still crisp. 6. Plate the baked cod with the tomato and olive sauce, accompanied by the steamed broccoli and carrots.

MEDITERRANEAN BARLEY SALAD

This Mediterranean Barley Salad is a hearty and flavorful dish that's perfect for a diabetic-friendly lunch. The barley provides a great source of fiber and whole grains, while the cherry tomatoes, olives, cucumber, and feta cheese add a variety of textures and Mediterranean flavors. The fresh oregano and tangy dressing bring everything together for a delicious and nutritious salad that's easy to make and full of healthy ingredients.

RECIPE 14	NUTRITIONAL VALUES (PER SERVING)			
Difficulty: Easy	**Calories:** 280	**Sodium:** 420mg	**Protein:** 8g	**Sugars:** 5g
Servings: 1	**Fiber:** 8g	**Carbohydrates:** 35g		**Fat:** 13g
Preparation Time: 10 minutes (plus time to cook barley)	**Cooking Time:** 0 minutes (assuming pre-cooked barley)		**Total Time:** 10 minutes	

INGREDIENTS	GUIDELINES
<ul><li>½ cup cooked barley</li><li>¼ cucumber, diced</li><li>¼ red bell pepper, diced</li><li>1 small tomato, diced</li><li>1 tablespoon red onion, finely chopped</li><li>1 tablespoon feta cheese, crumbled</li><li>1 tablespoon olives, sliced</li><li>1 tablespoon olive oil</li><li>1 teaspoon lemon juice</li><li>Salt and pepper to taste</li><li>Fresh herbs (such as parsley or mint), chopped</li></ul>	1. Cook the barley according to package instructions. Once cooked, let it cool to room temperature. 2. In a large salad bowl, combine the cooled barley, halved cherry tomatoes, halved olives, crumbled feta cheese, diced cucumber, and chopped fresh oregano. 3. In a small bowl, whisk together the olive oil, red wine vinegar, salt, and pepper to create the dressing. 4. Pour the dressing over the salad and toss gently to combine all the ingredients. 5. Taste and adjust the seasoning if necessary. You can add more salt, pepper, or vinegar to suit your taste. 6. Serve the salad at room temperature or chilled. It can be stored in the refrigerator for up to 2 days.

BAKED VEGETABLE RATATOUILLE

This Baked Vegetable Ratatouille is a colorful and healthy dish that's perfect for a diabetic-friendly meal. The combination of eggplant, zucchini, peppers, and tomatoes provides a variety of vitamins and antioxidants, while the thyme and garlic add depth of flavor. It's a simple and delicious way to enjoy a medley of vegetables in one dish. This ratatouille is a great option for a light dinner or as a side dish to complement any meal.

RECIPE 15	NUTRITIONAL VALUES (PER SERVING)			
Difficulty: Easy	**Calories:** 180	**Sodium:** 30mg	**Protein:** 3g	**Sugars:** 10g
Servings: 1	**Fiber:** 7g	**Carbohydrates:** 18g		**Fat:** 12g
Preparation Time: 15 minutes	**Cooking Time:** 35 minutes		**Total Time:** 50 minutes	

INGREDIENTS	GUIDELINES
<ul><li>¼ small eggplant, sliced</li><li>½ small zucchini, sliced</li><li>½ small yellow squash, sliced</li><li>¼ bell pepper (any color), sliced</li><li>½ small onion, sliced</li><li>1 garlic clove, minced</li><li>½ cup crushed tomatoes</li><li>1 tablespoon olive oil</li><li>¼ teaspoon dried thyme</li><li>¼ teaspoon dried basil</li><li>Salt and pepper to taste</li><li>Fresh basil or parsley, for garnish</li></ul>	1. Preheat your oven to 375°F (190°C). 2. In a large baking dish, layer the sliced eggplant, zucchini, bell peppers, and tomatoes, alternating and overlapping them in a circular pattern. 3. Sprinkle the minced garlic and fresh thyme leaves evenly over the top of the vegetables. 4. Drizzle the olive oil over the vegetables and season with salt and pepper. 5. Cover the baking dish with aluminum foil and bake in the preheated oven for 30 minutes. 6. Remove the foil and bake for an additional 15 minutes, or until the vegetables are tender and lightly browned. 7. Serve the ratatouille hot as a main dish or as a side to your favorite protein.

TURKEY & AVOCADO SALAD

This Turkey & Avocado Salad is a refreshing and nutritious option that is perfect for a light lunch or dinner. The combination of lean turkey breast and avocado provides a good balance of protein and healthy fats, making it both satisfying and heart-healthy. The cherry tomatoes and corn add a sweet pop of flavor and color, while the mixed greens serve as a crunchy base. This salad is not only delicious but also quick to prepare, ideal for a busy day when you want a meal that is both wholesome and hassle-free.

RECIPE 16	NUTRITIONAL VALUES (PER SERVING)			
Difficulty: Easy	**Calories:** 290	**Sodium:** 85mg	**Protein:** 25g	**Sugars:** 4g
Servings: 1	**Fiber:** 4g	**Carbohydrates:** 12g		**Fat:** 17g
Preparation Time: 10 minutes	**Cooking Time:** 0 minutes		**Total Time:** 10 minutes	

INGREDIENTS	GUIDELINES
<ul><li>3 ounces cooked turkey breast, sliced or shredded</li><li>½ ripe avocado, diced</li><li>½ cup mixed greens (such as spinach and arugula)</li><li>¼ cup cherry tomatoes, halved</li><li>1 tablespoon red onion, thinly sliced</li><li>1 tablespoon chopped nuts (such as almonds or walnuts)</li><li>1 tablespoon olive oil</li><li>1 tablespoon lemon juice</li><li>Salt and pepper to taste</li></ul>	1. In a large salad bowl, combine the mixed lettuce greens, sliced turkey breast, diced avocado, halved cherry tomatoes, and cooked corn kernels. 2. In a small bowl, whisk together the olive oil, lemon juice, salt, and pepper to create the dressing. 3. Pour the dressing over the salad and toss gently to coat all the ingredients evenly. 4. Taste and adjust the seasoning if necessary. You can add more lemon juice, salt, or pepper according to your preference. 5. Serve the salad immediately, while the ingredients are fresh, and the avocado is still vibrant.

VEGETABLE AND QUINOA OMELETTE

This Vegetable and Quinoa Omelette is a hearty and nutritious breakfast or brunch option that combines the goodness of eggs with the health benefits of quinoa and vegetables. The quinoa adds a unique texture and boosts the protein content, while the spinach, peppers, and onions provide essential vitamins and minerals. The feta cheese adds a tangy flavor that complements the fresh vegetables perfectly. This omelette is not only delicious and filling but also supports a balanced diabetic diet.

RECIPE 17	NUTRITIONAL VALUES (PER SERVING)			
Difficulty: Easy	**Calories:** 350	**Sodium:** 420mg	**Protein:** 20g	**Sugars:** 3g
Servings: 1	**Fiber:** 3g	**Carbohydrates:** 17g		**Fat:** 23g
Preparation Time: 10 minutes	**Cooking Time:** 10 minutes		**Total Time:** 20 minutes	

INGREDIENTS	GUIDELINES

INGREDIENTS

- 2 eggs
- ¼ cup cooked quinoa
- ¼ cup diced vegetables (such as bell peppers, spinach, and mushrooms)
- 1 tablespoon grated cheese (optional, choose a low-fat variety for a healthier option)
- 1 tablespoon olive oil
- Salt and pepper to taste

GUIDELINES

1. In a medium bowl, whisk the eggs until well beaten. Season with salt and pepper.
2. Heat 1 tablespoon of olive oil in a non-stick skillet over medium heat. Sauté the onion and bell pepper until they are soft and slightly caramelized, about 5 minutes.
3. Add the chopped spinach to the skillet and cook until it wilts, about 1-2 minutes.
4. Stir the cooked quinoa into the vegetable mixture in the skillet and spread the mixture evenly.
5. Pour the beaten eggs over the vegetables and quinoa. Tilt the pan to ensure the eggs evenly cover all the vegetables.
6. Sprinkle the crumbled feta cheese over the top of the omelette.
7. Cook the omelette over medium heat until the edges begin to lift from the pan and the bottom is set but the top is still slightly runny, about 3-4 minutes.
8. Carefully fold half of the omelette over itself using a spatula, then slide or flip the omelette to cook on the other side for another 2-3 minutes, until fully set.
9. Serve the omelette hot, cut into portions if desired.

TOFU BUDDHA BOWL

This Tofu Buddha Bowl is a vibrant and nutritious meal that combines a variety of textures and flavors. The crispy baked tofu provides a hearty protein source, while the mix of purple cabbage, carrots, and avocado offers a wealth of vitamins, minerals, and healthy fats. The quinoa serves as a wholesome base, rich in fiber and protein. Topped with crunchy sunflower seeds and drizzled with flavorful oils and soy sauce, this Buddha bowl is a fulfilling dish that's perfect for a healthy lunch or dinner, especially suited for a diabetic-friendly diet.

RECIPE 18	NUTRITIONAL VALUES (PER SERVING)			
Difficulty: Easy	**Calories:** 400	**Sodium:** 480mg	**Protein:** 18g	**Sugars:** 5g
Servings: 1	**Fiber:** 9g	**Carbohydrates:** 39g		**Fat:** 22g
Preparation Time: 15 minutes	**Cooking Time:** 20 minutes		**Total Time:** 35 minutes	

INGREDIENTS	GUIDELINES

INGREDIENTS

- ½ block of firm tofu, pressed and cubed
- ½ cup cooked brown rice or quinoa
- ½ cup broccoli florets
- ¼ cup shredded carrots
- ¼ cup sliced cucumber
- ¼ avocado, sliced
- 1 tablespoon soy sauce (low sodium)
- 1 teaspoon sesame oil
- 1 tablespoon olive oil
- 1 teaspoon sesame seeds
- Optional: 1 tablespoon hummus or tahini for dressing

GUIDELINES

1. Preheat the oven to 400°F (200°C). Line a baking sheet with parchment paper.
2. Toss the cubed tofu with olive oil, soy sauce, and a pinch of pepper. Spread the tofu cubes on the prepared baking sheet and bake for 15 minutes, turning halfway through until crispy and golden.
3. While the tofu is baking, prepare the vegetables. Cook the quinoa according to package instructions if not already prepared.
4. In a large bowl or individual serving bowls, start assembling the Buddha bowls. Divide the cooked quinoa evenly among the bowls.
5. Add the shredded purple cabbage, julienned carrots, and crispy tofu to each bowl.
6. Top each bowl with sliced avocado and sprinkle with sunflower seeds.
7. Drizzle with sesame oil and add a splash more soy sauce or tamari if desired.
8. Serve immediately, offering additional soy sauce or tamari on the side for extra seasoning.

BAKED SALMON WITH ASPARAGUS

This Baked Salmon with Asparagus is a healthy and flavorful dish that's perfect for a quick weeknight dinner or a nutritious lunch. The salmon provides a rich source of omega-3 fatty acids, which are beneficial for heart health, while the asparagus offers a good dose of fiber, vitamins, and minerals. The lemon and garlic add a fresh, zesty flavor that enhances the natural taste of the salmon and asparagus. This dish is not only simple to prepare but also aligns well with a diabetic-friendly diet, offering a balanced meal with high-quality protein and low carbohydrates.

RECIPE 19	NUTRITIONAL VALUES (PER SERVING)			
Difficulty: Easy	**Calories:** 340	**Sodium:** 75mg	**Protein:** 34g	**Sugars:** 2g
Servings: 1	**Fiber:** 3g	**Carbohydrates:** 6g		**Fat:** 20g
Preparation Time: 5 minutes	**Cooking Time:** 20 minutes		**Total Time:** 25 minutes	

INGREDIENTS	GUIDELINES
• 1 salmon fillet (about 4-6 ounces) • 5-6 asparagus spears, trimmed • 1 tablespoon olive oil • 1 tablespoon lemon juice • Salt and pepper to taste • **Optional:** 1 garlic clove, minced, or lemon slices for extra flavor	1. Preheat your oven to 400°F (200°C). Line a large baking sheet with parchment paper. 2. Arrange the asparagus in a single layer on the prepared baking sheet. Drizzle with 1 tablespoon of olive oil and sprinkle half of the minced garlic over the asparagus. Season with salt and pepper. 3. Place the salmon fillets on the baking sheet alongside the asparagus. Drizzle the remaining olive oil and the lemon juice over the salmon. Top each fillet with the remaining garlic and a few lemon slices. 4. Season the salmon with salt and pepper to taste. 5. Bake in the preheated oven for about 15-20 minutes, or until the salmon is cooked through and flakes easily with a fork and the asparagus is tender. 6. Serve immediately, garnished with additional lemon slices if desired.

PUMPKIN AND GINGER CREAM SOUP

This Pumpkin and Ginger Cream Soup is a comforting and nutritious dish, perfect for chilly days. The pumpkin provides a good source of vitamins A and C, while the ginger adds a warming and spicy note that complements the sweet pumpkin beautifully. The Greek yogurt incorporates a creamy texture and a boost of protein, making the soup even more satisfying. This soup is not only delicious and easy to prepare but also fits well into a diabetic-friendly diet, offering a balanced blend of nutrients.

RECIPE 20	NUTRITIONAL VALUES (PER SERVING)			
Difficulty: Easy	**Calories:** 150	**Sodium:** 300mg	**Protein:** 5g	**Sugars:** 8g
Servings: 1	**Fiber:** 4g	**Carbohydrates:** 18g		**Fat:** 7g
Preparation Time: 10 minutes	**Cooking Time:** 20 minutes		**Total Time:** 30 minutes	

INGREDIENTS	GUIDELINES
• 1 cup pumpkin puree (fresh or canned) • 1 cup vegetable broth • 1 tablespoon minced ginger • 1 garlic clove, minced • 1 tablespoon olive oil • ¼ cup coconut milk • Salt and pepper to taste	1. Heat the olive oil in a large pot over medium heat. Add the chopped onion and sauté until translucent, about 5 minutes. 2. Stir in the grated ginger and cook for another minute until fragrant. 3. Add the pumpkin puree and vegetable broth to the pot. Stir to combine and bring the mixture to a simmer. 4. Reduce the heat and let the soup simmer gently for about 15 minutes, allowing the flavors to meld together. 5. Remove the soup from heat. Using an immersion blender, blend the soup directly in the pot until smooth and creamy. Alternatively, you can transfer the soup to a blender and blend it in batches. 6. Stir in the Greek yogurt and season with salt and pepper to taste. Heat the soup gently if needed, but do not let it boil after adding the yogurt to avoid curdling. 7. Serve the soup hot, garnished with pumpkin seeds if desired. **Optional toppings:** pumpkin seeds, a swirl of cream, or fresh herbs

CHAPTER 8: DINNER

BEEF AND BELL PEPPER STIR-FRY

This Beef and Bell Pepper Stir-Fry is a vibrant and delicious meal that's quick and easy to prepare. It features thin slices of beef paired with colorful bell peppers, all coated in a savory sauce. This dish provides a good balance of protein and essential nutrients while being low in carbohydrates, making it well-suited for individuals managing diabetes.

RECIPE 1	NUTRITIONAL VALUES (PER SERVING)			
Difficulty: Easy	**Calories:** 450	**Sodium:** 430mg	**Protein:** 29g	**Sugars:** 4g
Servings: 1	**Fiber:** 2g	**Carbohydrates:** 8g		**Fat:** 34g
Preparation Time: 10 minutes	**Cooking Time:** 15 minutes		**Total Time:** 25 minutes	

INGREDIENTS	GUIDELINES
<ul><li>200 g of lean beef strips (such as sirloin or flank steak)</li><li>2 bell peppers, one red and one yellow, sliced</li><li>1 tablespoon sesame oil</li><li>2 cloves garlic, minced</li><li>1 piece of fresh ginger, minced</li><li>2 tablespoons reduced-sodium soy sauce</li><li>1 teaspoon olive oil</li><li>1 tablespoon red wine vinegar</li><li>1 teaspoon cornstarch dissolved in 2 tablespoons cold water</li><li>Freshly ground black pepper to taste</li></ul>	1. Heat 1 tablespoon of olive oil in a large skillet or wok over medium-high heat. 2. Add the minced garlic and ginger, sautéing until they become aromatic. 3. Increase the heat to high, add the beef strips and cook quickly until they are almost done. 4. Add the sliced bell peppers to the pan, continuing to cook, stirring frequently, until the peppers are just tender but still crisp. 5. Pour in the soy sauce and red wine vinegar. Add the sesame oil. 6. Stir in the cornstarch mixture and continue to cook until the sauce thickens slightly. 7. Once everything is cooked through, season with black pepper to taste.

LENTIL BURGER

This Lentil Burger offers a hearty, nutritious alternative to traditional meat burgers. Packed with protein and fiber from lentils and oats, it's a filling option that doesn't skimp on flavor, thanks to the inclusion of aromatic onions, garlic, and cumin. The whole wheat buns provide additional fiber, making this burger both satisfying and beneficial for blood sugar management. It's a fantastic meal choice for anyone looking for a delicious and healthy burger experience, especially those managing diabetes or following a vegetarian diet.

RECIPE 2	NUTRITIONAL VALUES (PER SERVING, INCLUDING BUN)			
Difficulty: Easy	**Calories:** 330	**Sodium:** 300mg	**Protein:** 18g	**Sugars:** 6g
Servings: 1	**Fiber:** 10g	**Carbohydrates:** 53g		**Fat:** 7g
Preparation Time: 15 minutes	**Cooking Time:** 10 minutes		**Total Time:** 25 minutes	

INGREDIENTS	GUIDELINES
<ul><li>½ cup cooked lentils</li><li>1 tablespoon breadcrumbs</li><li>1 tablespoon finely chopped onion</li><li>1 small clove garlic, minced</li><li>1 tablespoon chopped fresh parsley</li><li>1 egg white</li><li>Salt and pepper to taste</li><li>1 tablespoon olive oil</li></ul>	1. In a large bowl, mash the lentils until mostly smooth but with some texture remaining. 1. Stir in the rolled oats, chopped onion, minced garlic, and ground cumin. Season with salt and pepper. Mix until all ingredients are well combined. 2. Form the mixture into four patties. If the mixture is too moist, you can add a few more oats to help bind the ingredients. 3. Heat a few tablespoons of olive oil in a non-stick skillet over medium heat. Add the lentil patties and cook for about 4-5 minutes on each side, or until the patties are golden brown and firm. 4. Serve the lentil burgers on whole wheat buns with your choice of toppings such as lettuce, tomato slices, and pickles.

BEAN AND BLACK CABBAGE SOUP

This Bean and Black Cabbage Soup is a nourishing and hearty meal, perfect for colder days. It combines fiber-rich white beans and nutrient-dense black cabbage, resulting in a soup that's both filling and nutritious. The carrots, celery, and tomato add freshness and depth to the flavor, while the garlic provides a nice zing. This soup is ideal for anyone looking for a warming, diabetic-friendly dish that's rich in fiber and protein, helping to manage blood sugar levels. Enjoy it as a robust dinner or a comforting lunch option.

RECIPE 3	NUTRITIONAL VALUES (PER SERVING)			
Difficulty: Easy	**Calories:** 210	**Sodium:** 300mg	**Protein:** 12g	**Sugars:** 5g
Servings: 1	**Fiber:** 8g	**Carbohydrates:** 33g		**Fat:** 4g
Preparation Time: 10 minutes	**Cooking Time:** 20 minutes		**Total Time:** 30 minutes	

INGREDIENTS	GUIDELINES
<ul><li>½ cup canned cannellini beans, rinsed and drained</li><li>1 cup chopped black cabbage (also known as Tuscan kale or cavolo Nero)</li><li>1 small potato, peeled and diced</li><li>1 small carrot, diced</li><li>1 garlic clove, minced</li><li>1 tablespoon olive oil</li><li>2 cups vegetable broth</li><li>Salt and pepper to taste</li><li>A pinch of red pepper flakes (optional)</li><li>Grated Parmesan cheese for garnish (optional)</li></ul>	1. In a large pot, heat the olive oil over medium heat. Add the minced garlic and sauté until fragrant, about 1 minute. 1. Add the diced carrots and celery to the pot. Cook for about 5 minutes, stirring occasionally, until the vegetables begin to soften. 2. Stir in the diced tomato and cook for another 3 minutes. 3. Add the soaked and drained white beans along with the vegetable broth to the pot. Bring the mixture to a boil. 4. Once boiling, reduce the heat to a simmer and add the chopped black cabbage. Cover and let simmer for about 30 minutes, or until the beans are tender and the cabbage is wilted. 5. Season the soup with salt and pepper to taste. 6. Serve hot, garnished with grated Parmesan cheese if desired.

MUSHROOM AND SPINACH OMELETTE

This Mushroom and Spinach Omelette combines the earthy flavors of mushrooms with the freshness of spinach and the tangy taste of feta cheese, all enveloped in fluffy eggs. It's a nutritious and satisfying meal that is perfect for breakfast, brunch, or a light dinner. This omelette is not only delicious but also packed with proteins and vitamins, making it a fantastic choice for a healthy, balanced diet, particularly suitable for those managing diabetes.

RECIPE 4	NUTRITIONAL VALUES (PER SERVING)			
Difficulty: Easy	**Calories:** 320	**Sodium:** 420mg	**Protein:** 18g	**Sugars:** 3g
Servings: 1	**Fiber:** 2g	**Carbohydrates:** 8g		**Fat:** 24g
Preparation Time: 5 minutes	**Cooking Time:** 10 minutes		**Total Time:** 15 minutes	

INGREDIENTS	GUIDELINES
<ul><li>2 eggs</li><li>¼ cup sliced mushrooms</li><li>¼ cup fresh spinach, chopped</li><li>1 tablespoon grated cheese (optional, choose a low-fat variety for a healthier option)</li><li>1 tablespoon olive oil</li><li>Salt and pepper to taste</li></ul>	1. In a medium bowl, beat the eggs with salt and pepper until well mixed. Set aside. 2. Heat 1 tablespoon of olive oil in a non-stick skillet over medium heat. Add the onions and mushrooms, sautéing until the onions are translucent and the mushrooms are golden, about 5 minutes. 3. Add the spinach to the skillet and cook until just wilted, about 1-2 minutes. 4. Pour the beaten eggs evenly over the vegetables in the skillet. Let the eggs cook for a few seconds, then gently stir to distribute the vegetables evenly. 5. Reduce the heat to low and sprinkle the crumbled feta cheese over the omelette. 6. Cover and cook for about 4-5 minutes, or until the eggs are set and the bottom is golden. 7. Carefully fold the omelette in half with a spatula and slide onto a plate. 8. Serve the omelette hot, optionally garnished with additional feta or fresh herbs.

SESAME & BROCCOLI TOFU

This Sesame & Broccoli Tofu is a delightful and nutritious dish, perfect for a healthy dinner. The tofu provides a hearty base, offering a high-quality protein that's excellent for those managing their weight or blood sugar levels. The broccoli adds crunch and is packed with vitamins, while the sesame seeds give a nice textural contrast and a boost of minerals. This dish is flavorful with the aromatic presence of garlic and ginger, and the sesame oil ties all the flavors together beautifully. It's a simple yet satisfying meal that's quick to prepare and packed with health benefits.

RECIPE 5	NUTRITIONAL VALUES (PER SERVING)			
Difficulty: Easy	**Calories:** 190	**Sodium:** 330mg	**Protein:** 12g	**Sugars:** 2g
Servings: 1	**Fiber:** 3g	**Carbohydrates:** 8g		**Fat:** 14g
Preparation Time: 10 minutes	**Cooking Time:** 15 minutes		**Total Time:** 25 minutes	

INGREDIENTS	GUIDELINES
<ul><li>½ block of firm tofu, pressed and cubed</li><li>1 cup broccoli florets</li><li>1 tablespoon soy sauce (low sodium)</li><li>1 tablespoon sesame oil</li><li>1 teaspoon sesame seeds</li><li>1 garlic clove, minced</li><li>½ tablespoon ginger, grated</li><li>1 tablespoon olive oil</li></ul>	1. In a non-stick skillet or wok, heat a splash of olive oil over medium heat. Add the tofu cubes and fry until all sides are golden brown, about 5-7 minutes. Remove the tofu from the skillet and set aside. 2. In the same skillet, add the broccoli florets and a splash of water. Cover and let steam until the broccoli are bright green and tender, about 3-4 minutes. 3. Push the broccoli to the sides of the skillet and add the sesame oil to the center. Stir in the minced garlic and grated ginger, sautéing until fragrant, about 1 minute. 4. Return the tofu to the skillet. Add the soy sauce and toss everything together. Cook for another 2-3 minutes, allowing the flavors to meld. 5. Sprinkle sesame seeds over the tofu and broccoli mixture and give a final stir to combine. 6. Serve hot, garnished with additional sesame seeds or a drizzle of sesame oil if desired.

BEETROOT AND QUINOA SALAD

This Beetroot and Quinoa Salad is a vibrant and nutritious dish that combines the earthy flavors of beetroot with the nutty taste of quinoa. The arugula adds a peppery bite, while the walnuts provide a satisfying crunch. The goat cheese offers a creamy contrast to the other textures and flavors in the salad. Dressed with a simple balsamic vinaigrette, this salad is not only delicious but also packed with antioxidants, proteins, and healthy fats. It's an excellent choice for a light lunch or as a side dish for dinner, providing a balanced and satisfying meal that's especially suitable for those managing diabetes or seeking a heart-healthy diet.

RECIPE 6	NUTRITIONAL VALUES (PER SERVING)			
Difficulty: Easy	**Calories:** 320	**Sodium:** 200mg	**Protein:** 12g	**Sugars:** 7g
Servings: 1	**Fiber:** 5g	**Carbohydrates:** 30g		**Fat:** 18g
Preparation Time: 10 minutes (plus time for cooking quinoa if not pre-cooked)	**Cooking Time:** 0 minutes (assuming pre-cooked quinoa)		**Total Time:** 10 minutes	

INGREDIENTS	GUIDELINES
<ul><li>½ cup cooked quinoa</li><li>1 medium beetroot, cooked and diced</li><li>¼ cup arugula or mixed salad greens</li><li>1 tablespoon feta cheese, crumbled</li><li>1 tablespoon walnuts, chopped</li><li>1 tablespoon balsamic vinegar</li><li>1 tablespoon olive oil</li><li>Salt and pepper to taste</li></ul>	1. If starting with uncooked quinoa, rinse the quinoa under cold water, then cook according to package instructions. Typically, this involves combining the quinoa with water in a 2:1 ratio (water to quinoa), bringing it to a boil, then covering and simmering for about 15 minutes until the water is absorbed. Let it cool to room temperature. 2. In a large salad bowl, combine the cooked and cooled quinoa with the diced beetroots and arugula. 3. Add the chopped walnuts and crumbled goat cheese to the bowl. 4. In a small bowl, whisk together the balsamic vinegar and olive oil. Season the dressing with salt and pepper. 5. Drizzle the dressing over the salad and toss gently to ensure everything is evenly coated. 6. Serve the salad immediately or chill it in the refrigerator for about an hour before serving if you prefer it cold.

TURKEY AND SPINACH MEATBALLS

These Turkey and Spinach Meatballs are a healthy and flavorful twist on traditional meatballs. Incorporating spinach not only adds nutrients like iron and vitamins but also gives the meatballs a moist texture. The garlic, paprika, and rosemary add depth and a slight kick to the flavor profile. This dish is perfect for a protein-rich dinner that supports a balanced diet, particularly suitable for those managing diabetes or seeking nutritious meal options.

RECIPE 7	NUTRITIONAL VALUES (PER SERVING)			
Difficulty: Easy	**Calories:** 230	**Sodium:** 75mg	**Protein:** 27g	**Sugars:** 1g
Servings: 1	**Fiber:** 1g	**Carbohydrates:** 5g		**Fat:** 12g
Preparation Time: 15 minutes	**Cooking Time:** 20 minutes		**Total Time:** 35 minutes	

INGREDIENTS	GUIDELINES
<ul><li>4 ounces ground turkey</li><li>¼ cup fresh spinach, finely chopped</li><li>1 tablespoon grated Parmesan cheese</li><li>1 small clove garlic, minced</li><li>1 tablespoon onion, finely chopped</li><li>1 tablespoon breadcrumbs</li><li>1 egg white</li><li>Salt and pepper to taste</li><li>1 tablespoon olive oil</li></ul>	1. Preheat your oven to 375°F (190°C). Line a baking sheet with parchment paper or lightly grease it with olive oil. 2. In a large mixing bowl, combine the ground turkey, finely chopped spinach, chopped onion, minced garlic, paprika, rosemary, salt, and pepper. Mix well until all ingredients are evenly distributed. 3. Roll the mixture into 1-inch balls and place them on the prepared baking sheet. 4. Lightly brush the meatballs with olive oil to help them brown. 5. Bake in the preheated oven for 20 minutes, or until the meatballs are cooked through and slightly golden on the outside. 6. Serve the turkey and spinach meatballs hot. They can be paired with a dipping sauce like marinara or served over whole wheat pasta, or as part of a main meal with a side of vegetables.

GRILLED SWORDFISH WITH GREEN SAUCE

This Grilled Swordfish with Green Sauce is a delightful dish, perfect for a light and healthy dinner. The robust flavor of the swordfish pairs beautifully with the zesty and herby green sauce, enriched with the briny taste of capers and the freshness of parsley. The addition of lemon brings a bright acidity that balances the richness of the fish and olive oil. This meal is not only flavorful but also packed with healthy fats and proteins, making it a nutritious choice for those looking to maintain a balanced diet, particularly suitable for diabetic meal planning.

RECIPE 8	NUTRITIONAL VALUES (PER SERVING)			
Difficulty: Easy	**Calories:** 350	**Sodium:** 220mg	**Protein:** 34g	**Sugars:** 0g
Servings: 1	**Fiber:** 0g	**Carbohydrates:** 1g		**Fat:** 23g
Preparation Time: 10 minutes (plus marinating time if desired)	**Cooking Time:** 10 minutes		**Total Time:** 20 minutes	

INGREDIENTS	GUIDELINES
<ul><li>1 swordfish steak (about 6 ounces)</li><li>1 tablespoon olive oil</li><li>Salt and pepper to taste</li></ul>**For the Green Sauce:**<ul><li>1 small bunch of fresh parsley</li><li>1 clove garlic</li><li>1 tablespoon capers</li><li>1 tablespoon lemon juice</li><li>2 tablespoons olive oil</li><li>Salt to taste</li></ul>	7. Preheat your grill to medium-high heat. 8. In a small bowl, mix the chopped parsley, capers, minced garlic, olive oil, and lemon juice. Season with salt and pepper to taste. This will be your green sauce. 9. Brush the swordfish steaks lightly with olive oil and season both sides with salt and pepper. 10. Place the swordfish steaks on the hot grill and cook for about 4-5 minutes on each side, or until the fish is cooked through and shows clear grill marks. 11. Remove the swordfish from the grill and let it rest for a couple of minutes. 12. Serve the grilled swordfish steaks with the green sauce drizzled over the top or on the side for dipping.

CHICKEN CACCIATORE

This Chicken Cacciatore is a classic Italian dish that is both hearty and healthy. It features tender chicken breasts simmered in a rich tomato sauce with onions, bell peppers, and olives, all infused with aromatic herbs. This dish is perfect for a comforting dinner, providing a good balance of protein, fiber, and nutrients. The vibrant flavors and simple preparation make it a delightful choice for any weeknight meal, especially suitable for those managing diabetes.

RECIPE 9	NUTRITIONAL VALUES (PER SERVING)			
Difficulty: Easy	**Calories:** 290	**Sodium:** 590mg	**Protein:** 27g	**Sugars:** 6g
Servings: 1	**Fiber:** 4g	**Carbohydrates:** 15g		**Fat:** 12g
Preparation Time: 10 minutes	**Cooking Time:** 30 minutes		**Total Time:** 40 minutes	

INGREDIENTS

- 1 chicken thigh or breast (bone-in, skin-on for more flavor)
- ½ cup canned diced tomatoes
- ¼ onion, sliced
- 1 garlic clove, minced
- ¼ bell pepper, sliced
- ¼ cup mushrooms, sliced
- 1 tablespoon olive oil
- ¼ cup white wine (optional)
- ½ teaspoon dried oregano
- ½ teaspoon dried basil
- Salt and pepper to taste
- Fresh parsley, chopped, for garnish.

GUIDELINES

13. Heat olive oil in a large skillet over medium-high heat. Season the chicken breasts with salt and pepper, then add them to the skillet. Cook until browned on both sides, about 3-4 minutes per side. Remove the chicken from the skillet and set aside.
14. In the same skillet, add the sliced onions and bell peppers. Sauté until they start to soften, about 5 minutes. Add the minced garlic and sauté for an additional minute.
15. Return the chicken to the skillet. Add the diced tomatoes (with their juice), sliced olives, and dried Italian herbs. Stir to combine all the ingredients.
16. Reduce heat to medium-low, cover, and let simmer for 30-35 minutes, or until the chicken is cooked through and the vegetables are tender.
17. Taste and adjust seasoning with additional salt and pepper if needed.
18. Serve the chicken cacciatore hot, garnished with chopped fresh parsley.

CHICKEN AND VEGETABLE SOUP

This chicken and vegetable soup is a light and nutritious dish, perfect for a healthy and tasty meal. Prepared with fresh ingredients and rich in flavors, this soup is ideal for anyone looking to maintain stable blood sugar levels.

RECIPE 10	NUTRITIONAL VALUES (PER SERVING)			
Difficulty: Easy	**Calories:** 180	**Sodium:** 250mg	**Protein:** 20g	**Sugars:** 5g
Servings: 1	**Fiber:** 3g	**Carbohydrates:** 10g		**Fat:** 6g
Preparation Time: 10 minutes	**Cooking Time:** 20 minutes		**Total Time:** 30 minutes	

INGREDIENTS

- 1 skinless chicken breast, diced
- 1 small carrot, sliced
- 1 stalk celery, diced
- 1/4 small onion, chopped
- 1 clove garlic, minced
- 1/2 small zucchini, diced
- 1/4 cup broccoli florets
- 2 cups low-sodium chicken broth
- 1/2 tablespoon olive oil
- Salt and freshly ground black pepper, to taste
- Fresh chopped parsley, for garnish (optional)

GUIDELINES

1. In a small pot, heat the olive oil over medium heat.
2. Add the chopped onion and minced garlic, and sauté until they become translucent and fragrant, about 2-3 minutes.
3. Add the diced chicken breast and cook until it is golden brown on all sides.
4. Add the carrot, celery, zucchini, and broccoli. Stir well to combine the ingredients.
5. Pour the chicken broth into the pot and bring to a boil.
6. Reduce the heat and let the soup simmer for about 15-20 minutes, or until the vegetables are tender and the chicken is cooked through.
7. Taste the soup and adjust salt and pepper if needed.
8. Serve the soup hot, garnished with fresh chopped parsley if desired.

BULGUR BOWL WITH CHICKEN AND TZATZIKI

This Bulgur Bowl with Chicken and Tzatziki is a nutritious and satisfying meal that combines lean protein, whole grains, and a refreshing yogurt sauce. The bulgur provides a hearty base with a nutty flavor that complements the juicy grilled chicken perfectly. The homemade tzatziki adds a cool and creamy element, brightened with fresh cucumber, garlic, and mint. This dish is both flavorful and balanced, making it an ideal meal for anyone looking for a filling yet health-conscious option, especially suitable for those managing diabetes.

RECIPE 11	NUTRITIONAL VALUES (PER SERVING)			
Difficulty: Easy	**Calories:** 350	**Sodium:** 150mg	**Protein:** 28g	**Sugars:** 3g
Servings: 1	**Fiber:** 5g	**Carbohydrates:** 27g		**Fat:** 14g
Preparation Time: 15 minutes	**Cooking Time:** 20 minutes		**Total Time:** 35 minutes	

INGREDIENTS	GUIDELINES
<ul><li>½ cup cooked bulgur</li><li>1 small chicken breast (about 4-6 ounces)</li><li>1 tablespoon olive oil</li><li>Salt and pepper to taste</li><li>½ cup cucumber, diced</li><li>1 tablespoon red onion, finely chopped</li><li>¼ cup cherry tomatoes, halved</li><li>¼ cup tzatziki</li><li>A few fresh mint leaves, chopped (optional for garnish)</li></ul>	1. Cook the bulgur according to package instructions. Usually, this involves bringing water to a boil, adding the bulgur, reducing the heat, covering, and simmering until the water is absorbed and the grains are tender. Set aside to cool slightly. 2. For the tzatziki, mix the grated cucumber, Greek yogurt, minced garlic, chopped mint, and olive oil in a bowl. Season with salt and pepper to taste. Refrigerate until ready to use. 3. Grill the chicken breasts seasoned with salt and pepper, either on a grill or in a grill pan, until fully cooked and nicely charred. Let the chicken rest for a few minutes before slicing. 4. To assemble the bowls, divide the cooked bulgur among four bowls. Top each with sliced grilled chicken. 5. Spoon a generous amount of tzatziki over each serving. 6. Serve the bowls with lemon wedges on the side for squeezing.

CRUSTLESS VEGETABLE QUICHE

This Crustless Vegetable Quiche is a light and flavorful dish that is perfect for any meal of the day, from breakfast to dinner. Packed with protein-rich eggs and nutrient-dense vegetables like spinach, bell peppers, and onions, this quiche is both satisfying and healthy. The addition of low-fat cheese adds a delicious creamy texture without too much added fat, making this quiche an excellent option for those managing their weight or blood sugar levels. It's a versatile dish that can be adapted with various vegetables and cheeses to suit your taste.

RECIPE 12	NUTRITIONAL VALUES (PER SERVING)			
Difficulty: Easy	**Calories:** 230	**Sodium:** 400mg	**Protein:** 18g	**Sugars:** 4g
Servings: 1	**Fiber:** 2g	**Carbohydrates:** 8g		**Fat:** 15g
Preparation Time: 10 minutes	**Cooking Time:** 25 minutes		**Total Time:** 35 minutes	

INGREDIENTS	GUIDELINES
<ul><li>2 eggs</li><li>1/4 cup milk or cream</li><li>1/2 cup chopped vegetables (such as bell peppers, spinach, mushrooms, and onions)</li><li>1/4 cup grated cheese (such as cheddar or Swiss)</li><li>Salt and pepper to taste</li><li>1 tablespoon olive oil</li></ul>	1. Preheat your oven to 375°F (190°C). Lightly grease a 9-inch pie dish or similar baking dish with olive oil. 2. Heat olive oil in a skillet over medium heat. Add the chopped onion and diced bell pepper, sautéing until the onion is translucent and the pepper is soft, about 5 minutes. 3. Add the chopped spinach to the skillet and cook just until wilted, about 2 minutes. Remove from heat and let the vegetable mixture cool slightly. 4. In a large bowl, whisk the eggs until smooth. Stir in the cooled vegetable mixture and shredded cheese. Season with salt and pepper. 5. Pour the egg and vegetable mixture into the prepared baking dish, spreading it out evenly. 6. Bake in the preheated oven for 25 minutes, or until the quiche is set and the top is lightly golden. 7. Remove from the oven and let cool for a few minutes before slicing into wedges and serving.

MIXED GRILLED VEGETABLES

These Mixed Grilled Vegetables offer a colorful and tasty side dish that's perfect for any meal. Grilling brings out the natural sweetness and flavors of the vegetables, while the balsamic vinegar adds a tangy contrast. This dish is not only delicious but also packed with nutrients and fiber, making it an excellent choice for those looking to maintain a healthy and balanced diet. It's a versatile recipe that can be customized with your favorite vegetables or herbs to suit your preferences.

RECIPE 13	NUTRITIONAL VALUES (PER SERVING)			
Difficulty: Easy	**Calories:** 110	**Sodium:** 30mg	**Protein:** 3g	**Sugars:** 6g
Servings: 1	**Fiber:** 3g	**Carbohydrates:** 10g		**Fat:** 7g
Preparation Time: 10 minutes	**Cooking Time:** 15 minutes		**Total Time:** 25 minutes	

INGREDIENTS	GUIDELINES

- ¼ zucchini, sliced
- ¼ yellow squash, sliced
- ¼ bell pepper (any color), sliced
- ¼ eggplant, sliced
- 4 cherry tomatoes
- 1 tablespoon olive oil
- Salt and pepper to taste
- 1 teaspoon herbs de Provence or Italian seasoning

1. Preheat your grill to medium-high heat.
2. In a large bowl, toss the zucchini, bell peppers, asparagus, and mushrooms with olive oil, balsamic vinegar, salt, and pepper until everything is well coated.
3. Arrange the vegetables on the grill, either directly on the grates or using a grill basket to prevent smaller pieces from falling through.
4. Grill the vegetables for about 7-8 minutes on each side, turning occasionally, until they are tender and have charred marks.
5. Once grilled to your liking, remove the vegetables from the grill and serve them hot. You can sprinkle additional salt or drizzle more balsamic vinegar if desired.

CHICKEN CURRY WITH CAULIFLOWER RICE

This Chicken Curry with Cauliflower Rice is a light and flavorful dish that's perfect for those seeking a low-carbohydrate, high-protein meal. The curry-infused chicken paired with creamy coconut milk provides a rich and satisfying taste, while the cauliflower rice serves as a healthy, grain-free alternative to traditional rice, adding texture and fiber without the extra carbs. This dish is not only delicious but also fits well into a balanced diet, particularly suitable for diabetic meal plans or those looking to reduce carbohydrate intake.

RECIPE 14	NUTRITIONAL VALUES (PER SERVING)			
Difficulty: Easy	**Calories:** 350	**Sodium:** 120mg	**Protein:** 28g	**Sugars:** 5g
Servings: 1	**Fiber:** 4g	**Carbohydrates:** 15g		**Fat:** 20g
Preparation Time: 10 minutes	**Cooking Time:** 20 minutes		**Total Time:** 30 minutes	

INGREDIENTS	GUIDELINES

- 1 small chicken breast, cut into bite-sized pieces
- 1 cup cauliflower, grated or processed into rice-like grains
- ½ onion, finely chopped
- 1 garlic clove, minced
- ½ tablespoon curry powder
- ¼ teaspoon turmeric
- ¼ cup coconut milk
- 1 tablespoon olive oil
- Salt and pepper to taste
- Fresh cilantro for garnish

1. In a large skillet, heat 1 tablespoon of olive oil over medium heat. Add the chicken pieces and sprinkle them with curry powder, salt, and pepper. Cook until the chicken is golden brown and cooked through, about 8-10 minutes. Remove the chicken from the skillet and set aside.
2. In the same skillet, add the remaining tablespoon of olive oil. Add the cauliflower rice and sauté for about 5 minutes or until it starts to soften.
3. Return the cooked chicken to the skillet. Pour in the coconut milk and bring the mixture to a simmer. Let it cook for another 10 minutes, stirring occasionally, until the sauce thickens slightly.
4. Stir in the chopped coriander just before serving.
5. Serve the chicken curry over the cauliflower rice, garnishing with additional coriander if desired.

EGGPLANT CASSEROLE PARMIGIANA LIGHT

This Eggplant Casserole Parmigiana Light is a healthier version of the traditional Italian dish, offering a delicious combination of tender eggplant, tangy tomato sauce, and melted cheeses, all without the extra calories from frying. The use of light mozzarella and a moderate amount of Parmesan helps keep the fat content lower, while still providing a rich and satisfying flavor. The fresh basil adds a bright note to the dish, making it a perfect comfort food that's both nutritious and great for those managing their weight or looking for diabetic-friendly meals.

RECIPE 15	NUTRITIONAL VALUES (PER SERVING)			
Difficulty: Moderate	**Calories:** 180	**Sodium:** 320mg	**Protein:** 12g	**Sugars:** 9g
Servings: 1	**Fiber:** 6g	**Carbohydrates:** 18g		**Fat:** 8g
Preparation Time: 15 minutes	**Cooking Time:** 30 minutes		**Total Time:** 45 minutes	

INGREDIENTS	GUIDELINES

INGREDIENTS

- 1 small eggplant, sliced into ½-inch rounds
- 1 cup canned crushed tomatoes
- 1 clove garlic, minced
- ¼ cup shredded mozzarella cheese (low-fat for a lighter version)
- 1 tablespoon grated Parmesan cheese
- 1 teaspoon dried basil
- 1 teaspoon dried oregano
- Salt and pepper to taste
- Olive oil spray (for a lighter option)

GUIDELINES

1. Preheat your oven to 375°F (190°C). Lightly grease a baking dish with olive oil spray.
2. Arrange the eggplant slices in a single layer on a baking sheet. Lightly spray with olive oil and season with salt and pepper. Bake for 15 minutes, flipping halfway through, until the eggplant is tender and beginning to brown.
3. In a small saucepan, heat the crushed peeled tomatoes over medium heat. Simmer for 10 minutes, seasoning with salt and pepper.
4. To assemble the casserole, spread a thin layer of the tomato sauce on the bottom of the prepared baking dish. Layer half of the baked eggplant slices over the sauce. Sprinkle with half of the mozzarella and some of the chopped basil.
5. Repeat with another layer of tomato sauce, the remaining eggplant slices, and the remaining mozzarella. Top with grated Parmesan cheese.
6. Cover with aluminum foil and bake in the preheated oven for 25 minutes. Remove the foil and bake for an additional 10 minutes, or until the cheese is bubbly and golden.
7. Let the casserole cool for 10 minutes before serving. Garnish with fresh basil.

CORN TORTILLAS WITH BLACK BEANS AND SAUCE

This recipe for Corn Tortillas with Black Beans and Sauce is a simple yet delicious meal that's perfect for a quick lunch or dinner. The black beans provide a good source of protein and fiber, making them very filling and beneficial for blood sugar management. The fresh tomato and avocado sauce add a vibrant, fresh flavor and healthy fats, while the lime and coriander bring a bright citrusy and herby punch. This dish is not only nutritious but also very versatile, allowing for various additional toppings to suit your taste preferences. It's a delightful, heart-healthy option ideal for anyone looking for a satisfying vegetarian meal.

RECIPE 16	NUTRITIONAL VALUES (PER SERVING, 2 FILLED TORTILLAS)			
Difficulty: Easy	**Calories:** 280	**Sodium:** 200mg	**Protein:** 9g	**Sugars:** 3g
Servings: 1	**Fiber:** 11g	**Carbohydrates:** 45g		**Fat:** 8g
Preparation Time: 10 minutes	**Cooking Time:** 10 minutes		**Total Time:** 20 minutes	

INGREDIENTS	GUIDELINES

INGREDIENTS

- 2 corn tortillas
- ½ cup black beans, cooked and drained
- ¼ cup tomato sauce
- 1 small onion, chopped
- 1 clove garlic, minced
- ¼ teaspoon cumin
- ¼ teaspoon chili powder
- Salt and pepper to taste
- 1 tablespoon olive oil

Optional toppings: shredded cheese, chopped cilantro, diced avocado

GUIDELINES

1. Heat the corn tortillas on a skillet over medium heat until warm and slightly crispy, about 1 minute on each side. Keep them warm by wrapping in a cloth or placing in a tortilla keeper.
2. In a medium saucepan, heat the black beans over medium heat. Season with salt and pepper and cook until heated through, about 5 minutes.
3. Prepare the sauce by mixing the diced tomatoes, diced avocado, chopped coriander, and lime juice in a bowl. Season with salt and pepper to taste.
4. To assemble, place two warm tortillas on each plate. Spoon the heated black beans onto each tortilla, followed by a generous scoop of the tomato-avocado sauce.
5. Add any additional toppings such as onions, jalapeños, or lettuce if desired.
6. Serve immediately, allowing each person to fold their tortillas into tacos.

BAKED CAULIFLOWER STEAK

This Baked Cauliflower Steak recipe offers a hearty, satisfying dish that's perfect for those seeking a plant-based alternative to traditional steaks. The smoked paprika and garlic powder gives the cauliflower a robust flavor, while the lemon juice adds a refreshing zest that complements the spices beautifully. Topped with fresh parsley, these cauliflower steaks are not only flavorful but also visually appealing. They make a fantastic centerpiece for a vegetarian meal or a unique side dish for meat eaters. The simplicity of preparation combined with the health benefits of cauliflower—rich in vitamins, minerals, and fiber—makes this dish a nutritious choice for any meal.

RECIPE 17	NUTRITIONAL VALUES (PER SERVING)		
Difficulty: Easy	**Calories:** 120	**Sodium:** 150mg	**Protein:** 3g	**Sugars:** 4g
Servings: 1	**Fiber:** 4g	**Carbohydrates:** 10g	**Fat:** 9g
Preparation Time: 5 minutes	**Cooking Time:** 25 minutes	**Total Time:** 30 minutes

INGREDIENTS	GUIDELINES

- 1 large cauliflower slice (about 1-inch thick from a large head)
- 1 tablespoon olive oil
- Salt and pepper to taste
- 1 teaspoon garlic powder
- 1 teaspoon smoked paprika

Optional: Fresh herbs or a squeeze of lemon for garnish

1. Preheat your oven to 400°F (200°C). Line a baking sheet with parchment paper.
2. Remove the leaves from the cauliflower and trim the stem so the cauliflower can sit flat. Slice the cauliflower into 3/4-inch-thick steaks. Depending on the size of your cauliflower, you can get about 3-4 steaks from one head.
3. In a small bowl, mix the olive oil, lemon juice, smoked paprika, garlic powder, salt, and pepper.
4. Brush both sides of each cauliflower steak with the olive oil mixture. Place the steaks on the prepared baking sheet.
5. Bake in the preheated oven for about 12-15 minutes on each side, or until the cauliflower is tender and the edges are crispy and browned.
6. Serve the cauliflower steaks garnished with lemon zest and fresh parsley.

SHRIMP AND VEGETABLE SKEWERS

These Shrimp and Vegetable Skewers are a delightful mix of juicy prawns and fresh vegetables, all enhanced by a simple, flavorful marinade. The skewers make a perfect dish for a quick summer barbecue or a healthy, easy-to-prepare meal any time of the year. They offer a high-protein, low-carbohydrate option suitable for a balanced diet, including for those managing diabetes. The vibrant colors and charred edges from grilling make these skewers not only tasty but also visually appealing.

RECIPE 18	NUTRITIONAL VALUES (PER SERVING)		
Difficulty: Easy	**Calories:** 200	**Sodium:** 150mg	**Protein:** 24g	**Sugars:** 4g
Servings: 1	**Fiber:** 2g	**Carbohydrates:** 10g	**Fat:** 8g
Preparation Time: 15 minutes (plus marinating time)	**Cooking Time:** 10 minutes	**Total Time:** 25 minutes

INGREDIENTS	GUIDELINES

- 6 large shrimp, peeled and deveined
- ¼ bell pepper, cut into chunks
- ¼ zucchini, sliced into rounds
- ¼ onion, cut into chunks
- 1 tablespoon olive oil
- 1 garlic clove, minced
- 1 tablespoon lemon juice
- Salt and pepper to taste

Optional: 1 teaspoon dried herbs (like oregano or basil) or chili flakes for extra flavor

1. In a large bowl, combine the lemon juice, minced garlic, olive oil, salt, and pepper. Mix well to create the marinade.
2. Add the prawns to the marinade and toss to coat. Cover and refrigerate for at least 30 minutes to allow the flavors to meld.
3. If using wooden skewers, soak them in water for at least 20 minutes to prevent burning.
4. Preheat your grill to medium-high heat.
5. Thread the marinated prawns, bell pepper pieces, zucchini slices, and onion chunks alternately onto the skewers.
6. Grill the skewers for 2-3 minutes on each side or until the prawns are pink and cooked through, and the vegetables are slightly charred and tender.
7. Serve the skewers hot, garnished with fresh lemon wedges for squeezing over the shrimp and vegetables.

POLENTA WITH MUSHROOM RAGOUT

This Polenta with Mushroom Ragout is a comforting and hearty dish perfect for a cozy dinner. The creamy polenta serves as a smooth base that complements the rich flavors of the savory mushroom ragout, enhanced with rosemary and garlic. Porcini mushrooms offer a deep umami taste that enriches the simple polenta, making this meal not only delicious but also visually appealing. The addition of Parmesan cheese adds a salty, nutty flavor that ties all the elements together beautifully. This dish is sure to satisfy both vegetarians and meat-eaters alike, offering a wholesome and flavorful dining experience.

RECIPE 19	NUTRITIONAL VALUES (PER SERVING)			
Difficulty: Intermediate	**Calories:** 350	**Sodium:** 450mg	**Protein:** 12g	**Sugars:** 4g
Servings: 1		**Fiber:** 4g	**Carbohydrates:** 45g	**Fat:** 14g
Preparation Time: 10 minutes		**Cooking Time:** 20 minutes		**Total Time:** 30 minutes

INGREDIENTS	GUIDELINES
<ul><li>½ cup instant polenta</li><li>1 ½ cups water</li><li>1 tablespoon butter</li><li>Salt and pepper, to taste</li><li>1 tablespoon olive oil</li><li>1 clove garlic, minced</li><li>1 cup sliced mushrooms (such as cremini or button)</li><li>½ cup diced tomatoes</li><li>¼ cup vegetable broth</li><li>1 tablespoon chopped fresh parsley</li><li>Grated Parmesan cheese, for serving</li></ul>	1. In a medium saucepan, bring water or vegetable broth to a boil. Gradually whisk in the polenta. Reduce the heat to low and continue stirring often, until the polenta thickens and is creamy, about 20-30 minutes. 2. While the polenta is cooking, heat olive oil in a large skillet over medium heat. Add the minced garlic and sauté until fragrant, about 1 minute. 3. Add the sliced mushrooms to the skillet and cook until they begin to brown and release their juices, about 5-7 minutes. 4. Stir in the diced tomatoes and chopped rosemary. Season with salt and pepper. Let the mixture simmer for about 10 minutes, until it thickens into a ragout. 5. Once the polenta is cooked and creamy, stir in the grated Parmesan cheese and adjust seasoning with salt and pepper. 6. To serve, spoon the creamy polenta onto plates and top with a generous portion of mushroom ragout. 7. Garnish with additional Parmesan cheese and a sprig of rosemary if desired.

BLACK RICE AND EDAMAME BOWL

This Black Rice and Edamame Bowl is a vibrant and nutritious dish that combines the nutty flavor of black rice with the fresh, green taste of edamame. The addition of crunchy carrots, creamy avocado, and pumpkin seeds provides a variety of textures and flavors that enhance the overall experience. The soy sauce and sesame oil dressing add a savory umami element that ties all the ingredients together beautifully. This bowl is not only visually appealing but also packed with nutrients, making it a perfect choice for a healthy, filling meal that is easy to prepare and delicious to eat.

RECIPE 20	NUTRITIONAL VALUES (PER SERVING)			
Difficulty: Easy	**Calories:** 320	**Sodium:** 510mg	**Protein:** 10g	**Sugars:** 3g
Servings: 1		**Fiber:** 7g	**Carbohydrates:** 45g	**Fat:** 12g
Preparation Time: 5 minutes (assuming pre-cooked rice)		**Cooking Time:** 5 minutes		**Total Time:** 10 minutes

INGREDIENTS	GUIDELINES
<ul><li>½ cup cooked black rice</li><li>½ cup shelled edamame (cooked)</li><li>¼ cup shredded carrots</li><li>¼ cup sliced cucumber</li><li>1 green onion, chopped</li><li>1 tablespoon soy sauce (low sodium)</li><li>1 teaspoon sesame oil</li><li>1 teaspoon rice vinegar</li><li>1 teaspoon sesame seeds</li></ul>	1. Rinse the black rice under cold water until the water runs clear. Combine the rinsed rice and water in a pot and bring to a boil. Once boiling, reduce the heat to low, cover, and let it simmer for about 30 minutes, or until the water is absorbed and the rice is tender. 2. While the rice is cooking, prepare the vegetables and other ingredients. Cook the edamame according to package instructions if they are not already prepared. 3. Once the rice is cooked, let it cool slightly. In a large mixing bowl, combine the cooked black rice, cooked edamame, grated carrot, diced avocado, and pumpkin seeds. 4. In a small bowl, whisk together the soy sauce and sesame oil. Drizzle this dressing over the rice mixture and toss gently to combine. Season with salt and pepper to taste. 5. Divide the rice mixture among bowls. Serve immediately or at room temperature.

CHAPTER 9: SNACKS AND SNACKS

SPINACH AND BLUEBERRY PROTEIN SHAKE

This Spinach and Blueberry Protein Shake is a quick and nutritious snack that combines the health benefits of leafy greens and berries with the muscle-building power of protein. Ideal for a post-workout refreshment or a midday pick-me-up, this shake not only fuels your body but also pleases your taste buds with its blend of natural sweetness and creamy texture. The antioxidants in blueberries and the vitamins in spinach make this shake a powerful ally for your health and wellness goals.

RECIPE 1	NUTRITIONAL VALUES (PER SERVING)			
Difficulty: Easy	**Calories:** 180	**Sodium:** 180mg	**Protein:** 20g	**Sugars:** 10g
Servings: 1	**Fiber:** 4g	**Carbohydrates:** 18g		**Fat:** 3g
Preparation Time: 5 minutes	**Cooking Time:** 0 minutes		**Total Time:** 5 minutes	

INGREDIENTS	GUIDELINES
<ul><li>1 cup fresh spinach</li><li>1/2 cup blueberries (fresh or frozen)</li><li>1 scoop protein powder (vanilla or unflavored)</li><li>1 cup unsweetened almond milk</li></ul>	1. Place the spinach, blueberries, protein powder, and almond milk in a blender. 2. Blend on high until smooth and creamy. If the shake is too thick, add a little more almond milk until you reach the desired consistency. 3. Taste and adjust the sweetness if necessary. Depending on your protein powder, you might want to add a teaspoon of honey or a few drops of stevia if more sweetness is needed. 4. Pour the shake into a glass and serve immediately. For an extra touch, you can garnish with a few blueberries or a sprinkle of chia seeds.

CARROT AND HUMMUS STICKS

This Carrot and Hummus Sticks snack is incredibly simple yet nutritious and satisfying. It combines the natural sweetness and crunch of carrots with the creamy, savory taste of hummus, providing a balanced snack rich in fiber, protein, and healthy fats. Ideal for a quick midday snack, a healthy addition to a lunchbox, or a perfect party appetizer, this duo is not only delicious but also great for promoting fullness and supporting overall health.

RECIPE 2	NUTRITIONAL VALUES (PER SERVING)			
Difficulty: Easy	**Calories:** 180	**Sodium:** 300mg	**Protein:** 6g	**Sugars:** 6g
Servings: 1	**Fiber:** 6g	**Carbohydrates:** 24g		**Fat:** 8g
Preparation Time: 5 minutes	**Cooking Time:** 0 minutes		**Total Time:** 5 minutes	

INGREDIENTS	GUIDELINES
<ul><li>1 medium carrot</li><li>2 tablespoons hummus</li></ul>	1. Wash, peel, and slice the carrots into stick-like shapes, approximately 3-4 inches long and 1/2 inch thick. This size is ideal for dipping. 2. Serve the carrot sticks alongside a bowl of hummus. You can use any flavor of hummus you prefer, such as classic, roasted red pepper, or garlic. 3. To enhance the snack, you can sprinkle the hummus with a bit of paprika, olive oil, or chopped parsley for added flavor and visual appeal.

SEED AND NUT CRACKERS

This crunchy snack is especially suitable for diabetics, as it's rich in fiber and healthy fats with very few net carbohydrates. Perfect as a snack or paired with cheeses or hummus.

RECIPE 3	NUTRITIONAL VALUES (PER SERVING)			
Difficulty: Easy	**Calories:** 200	**Sodium:** 150mg	**Protein:** 8g	**Sugars:** 1g
Servings: 1	**Fiber:** 5g	**Carbohydrates:** 10g		**Fat:** 15g
Preparation Time: 10 minutes	**Cooking Time:** 15 minutes		**Total Time:** 25 minutes	

INGREDIENTS	GUIDELINES
<ul><li>2 tablespoons of flax seeds</li><li>2 tablespoons of sunflower seeds</li><li>2 tablespoons of pumpkin seeds</li><li>1 tablespoon of chopped nuts</li><li>1 egg white</li><li>A pinch of sea salt</li></ul>	1. Preheat the oven to 350°F (180°C) and line a baking tray with parchment paper. 2. In a bowl, mix all the seeds and chopped nuts. 3. Add the egg white and sea salt to the seed and nut mixture, stirring well to ensure everything is evenly coated. 4. Spread the mixture on the prepared tray, pressing down to form a thin, even layer. 5. Bake in the oven for about 15 minutes, or until the crackers are golden and crispy. 6. Allow to cool completely before breaking into irregular pieces.

AVOCADO TOAST WITH POACHED EGG

This delightful recipe combines the creamy texture of ripe avocado with the gentle richness of a perfectly poached egg, all atop a crispy slice of whole grain toast. The combination of heart-healthy fats from the avocado and high-quality protein from the egg makes this dish not only a treat for the taste buds but also a powerhouse of nutrition. Sprinkled with just a pinch of salt and pepper, each bite offers a perfect balance of savory flavors that melt in your mouth. This avocado toast with poached egg is an ideal choice for a nutritious breakfast, a quick and satisfying lunch, or even a light dinner. It's a simple, elegant meal that's quick to prepare but rich in both taste and health benefits.

RECIPE 4	NUTRITIONAL VALUES (PER SERVING)			
Difficulty: Medium	**Calories:** 300	**Sodium:** 300mg	**Protein:** 12g	**Sugars:** 3g
Servings: 1	**Fiber:** 7g	**Carbohydrates:** 30g		**Fat:** 17g
Preparation Time: 5 minutes	**Cooking Time:** 5 minutes		**Total Time:** 10 minutes	

INGREDIENTS	GUIDELINES
<ul><li>1 slice of whole grain bread</li><li>½ avocado</li><li>1 egg</li><li>Salt and pepper to taste</li></ul>	1. Begin by toasting the whole grain bread to a golden-brown crispness, ensuring it offers a sturdy base with a satisfying crunch. 2. Meanwhile, mash the half avocado until creamy and spread it evenly over the toasted bread, creating a rich, green layer. 3. Poach the egg to your liking, aiming for a firm white and a yolk that still boasts a gentle flow when pierced. 4. Gently lay the poached egg atop the avocado spread, the warmth of the egg slightly melding into the cool avocado. 5. Season with a light sprinkling of salt and a twist of freshly ground pepper to enhance the natural flavors of the dish. 6. Serve immediately to enjoy the contrast of warm egg and cool, creamy avocado on crunchy toast.

BAKED ZUCCHINI CHIPS

These baked zucchini chips are a light and crispy snack, ideal for those looking for a healthy alternative to fried potato chips. They are low in carbohydrates and high in fiber, great for maintaining stable blood sugar levels.

RECIPE 5	NUTRITIONAL VALUES (PER SERVING)			
Difficulty: Easy	**Calories:** 120	**Sodium:** 40mg	**Protein:** 3g	**Sugars:** 7g
Servings: 1	**Fiber:** 3g	**Carbohydrates:** 10g		**Fat:** 9g
Preparation Time: 10 minutes	**Cooking Time:** 20 minutes		**Total Time:** 30 minutes	

INGREDIENTS	GUIDELINES
<ul><li>2 medium zucchinis</li><li>1 tablespoon of olive oil</li><li>Salt and pepper to taste</li><li>Choice of spices</li></ul>	1. Preheat the oven to 425°F (220°C) and line a baking sheet with parchment paper. 2. Slice the zucchinis into thin rounds, trying to keep them uniform for even cooking. 3. In a large bowl, mix the zucchini slices with olive oil, salt, pepper, and your chosen spices. 4. Arrange the zucchini slices in a single layer on the prepared baking sheet, ensuring they do not overlap. 5. Bake in the oven for 10 minutes, then flip the chips and continue baking for another 8-10 minutes or until they are crispy and golden. 6. Remove from the oven and let cool on a plate lined with paper towels to remove excess oil. 7. Serve immediately to enjoy their crispiness.

GREEK YOGURT AND BERRY PARFAIT

These baked zucchini chips are a light and crispy snack, ideal for those looking for a healthy alternative to fried potato chips. They are low in carbohydrates and high in fiber, great for maintaining stable blood sugar levels.

RECIPE 6	NUTRITIONAL VALUES (PER SERVING)			
Difficulty: Easy	**Calories:** 150	**Sodium:** 50mg	**Protein:** 12g	**Sugars:** 12g
Servings: 1	**Fiber:** 3g	**Carbohydrates:** 18g		**Fat:** 6g
Preparation Time: 5 minutes	**Cooking Time:** 0 minutes		**Total Time:** 5 minutes	

INGREDIENTS	GUIDELINES
<ul><li>½ cup Greek yogurt, unsweetened</li><li>½ cup mixed berries (blueberries, strawberries)</li><li>1 tablespoon chopped nuts (almonds or walnuts)</li></ul>	1. In a serving glass, layer the Greek yogurt followed by a layer of mixed berries. 2. Repeat the layers until all ingredients are used. 3. Top with chopped nuts for a crunchy finish.

CHEESE AND OLIVE STUFFED CHERRY TOMATOES

Cheese and Olive Stuffed Cherry Tomatoes offer a burst of Mediterranean flavors in a tiny package. This snack is not only tasty but also visually appealing, perfect for a light bite.

RECIPE 7	NUTRITIONAL VALUES (PER SERVING)			
Difficulty: Easy	**Calories:** 100	**Sodium:** 200mg	**Protein:** 2g	**Sugars:** 3g
Servings: 1	**Fiber:** 1g	**Carbohydrates:** 5g		**Fat:** 8g
Preparation Time: 10 minutes	**Cooking Time:** 0 minutes		**Total Time:** 10 minutes	

INGREDIENTS	GUIDELINES
<ul><li>5 cherry tomatoes</li><li>1 tablespoon cream cheese</li><li>5 small pitted olives, finely chopped</li><li>Fresh basil for garnish</li></ul>	1. Slice off the top of each cherry tomato and scoop out the insides with a small spoon. 2. In a small bowl, mix the cream cheese and chopped olives. 3. Stuff each tomato with the cream cheese mixture. 4. Garnish with a small basil leaf. 5. Serve immediately or chill before serving.

CELERY BOATS WITH PEANUT BUTTER

These Celery Boats with Peanut Butter, often referred to as "ants on a log" when using smaller raisin amounts, are a classic and fun snack that's perfect for both children and adults. This simple combination of crispy celery filled with creamy peanut butter and topped with sweet raisins provides a good balance of fiber, protein, and healthy fats. It's a satisfying, nutritious snack that's quick to prepare and can be easily customized. For a twist, try using different types of nut butter or toppings like chopped nuts or dried cranberries for added flavor and texture.

RECIPE 8	NUTRITIONAL VALUES (PER SERVING, 1 FILLED STALK)			
Difficulty: Easy	**Calories:** 150	**Sodium:** 100mg	**Protein:** 6g	**Sugars:** 8g
Servings: 1	**Fiber:** 2g	**Carbohydrates:** 12g		**Fat:** 10g
Preparation Time: 5 minutes	**Cooking Time:** 0 minutes		**Total Time:** 5 minutes	

INGREDIENTS	GUIDELINES
<ul><li>2 large celery stalks</li><li>2 tablespoons peanut butter</li></ul>**Optional toppings:** raisins, dried cranberries, or chopped nuts	1. Cut the celery stalks into pieces about 3 to 4 inches long. 2. Spread a generous amount of peanut butter into the groove of each celery piece. 3. Sprinkle raisins evenly over the peanut butter-filled celery to create "boats." 4. Serve immediately or chill in the refrigerator for a refreshing snack.

CINNAMON APPLE CHIPS

Cinnamon Apple Chips are a delicious and healthy snack that combines the natural sweetness of apples with the warm spice of cinnamon. This simple treat is perfect for satisfying your sweet tooth without any added sugars. The lemon juice not only helps to prevent browning but also adds a slight tangy flavor that complements the cinnamon well. These apple chips are great for snacking on their own, or you can use them as toppings for salads, oatmeal, or yogurt, adding a delightful crunch and flavor.

RECIPE 9	NUTRITIONAL VALUES (PER SERVING)			
Difficulty: Easy	**Calories:** 95	**Sodium:** 2mg	**Protein:** 0.5g	**Sugars:** 19g
Servings: 1	**Fiber:** 4g	**Carbohydrates:** 25g		**Fat:** 0g
Preparation Time: 10 minutes	**Cooking Time:** 2 hours		**Total Time:** 2 hours 10 minutes	

INGREDIENTS	GUIDELINES
• 1 large apple (such as Fuji or Honeycrisp) • ½ teaspoon ground cinnamon **Optional:** a sprinkle of sugar or sugar substitute for extra sweetness	1. Preheat your oven to 200°F (93°C). Line two baking sheets with parchment paper. 2. Wash the apples and thinly slice them using a mandoline slicer or a sharp knife. Aim for slices about 1/8 inch thick. Remove any seeds from the slices. 3. In a large bowl, toss the apple slices with lemon juice to prevent browning. 4. Arrange the apple slices in a single layer on the prepared baking sheets. Sprinkle the slices evenly with ground cinnamon. 5. Bake in the preheated oven for 1 hour. Flip the apple slices over and continue baking for another hour, or until the apple slices are dried out but still pliable. If you prefer crisper chips, extend the baking time by 30-60 minutes, checking frequently to prevent burning. 6. Remove the apple chips from the oven and let them cool completely on the baking sheets. They will continue to crisp up as they cool. 7. Store the cooled apple chips in an airtight container at room temperature for up to a week.

OAT AND CHIA SEED BARS

Homemade bars with oats, chia seeds, and mixed dried fruit, an excellent source of slow-release energy, ideal for diabetics.

RECIPE 10	NUTRITIONAL VALUES (PER SERVING)			
Difficulty: Medium	**Calories:** 250	**Sodium:** 180mg	**Protein:** 6g	**Sugars:** 10g
Servings: 1	**Fiber:** 4g	**Carbohydrates:** 38g		**Fat:** 10g
Preparation Time: 15 minutes	**Cooking Time:** 20 minutes		**Total Time:** 35 minutes	

INGREDIENTS	GUIDELINES
• ½ cup of rolled oats • 1 tablespoon of chia seeds • 1 tablespoon of honey • ¼ cup of mixed dried fruit, chopped	1. Preheat the oven to 350°F (175°C). 2. In a bowl, combine all ingredients and mix well. 3. Press the mixture into a small baking dish lined with parchment paper. 4. Bake for about 20 minutes or until golden. 5. Allow to cool completely before cutting into bars.

CHAPTER 10: DESSERTS AND SWEETS

OATMEAL AND APPLE BISCUITS

These Oatmeal and Apple Biscuits are a wholesome and delightful treat that combines apples' natural sweetness and oats' heartiness. Infused with the warm spice of cinnamon and the richness of eggs, these biscuits are both nutritious and satisfying. They are perfect for a quick breakfast, a healthy snack, or a light dessert. Easy to make and naturally sweetened, these biscuits are a great way to enjoy a guilt-free sweet treat while still catering to health-conscious preferences.

RECIPE 1	NUTRITIONAL VALUES (PER BISCUIT, IF USING HONEY)			
Difficulty: Easy	**Calories:** 100	**Sodium:** 15mg	**Protein:** 3g	**Sugars:** 6g
Servings: 1 makes about 4-5 small biscuits	**Fiber:** 2g	**Carbohydrates:** 17g		**Fat:** 2g
Preparation Time: 10 minutes	**Cooking Time:** 15 minutes		**Total Time:** 25 minutes	

INGREDIENTS	GUIDELINES
<ul><li>½ cup rolled oats</li><li>¼ cup whole wheat flour</li><li>1 small apple, peeled and finely grated</li><li>1 tablespoon honey or maple syrup</li><li>1 tablespoon unsalted butter, melted</li><li>¼ teaspoon cinnamon</li><li>¼ teaspoon baking powder</li><li>A pinch of salt</li></ul>	1. Preheat your oven to 350°F (175°C). Line a baking sheet with parchment paper. 2. In a large mixing bowl, combine the rolled oats, finely chopped apple, and cinnamon. 3. In a separate small bowl, beat the eggs with the sweetener until well mixed. 4. Pour the egg and sweetener mixture into the oat and apple mixture. Stir until all ingredients are thoroughly combined and the mixture holds together. The mixture should be sticky and hold its shape when pressed. 5. Scoop about a tablespoon of the mixture onto the prepared baking sheet for each biscuit. Flatten them slightly with the back of the spoon to form rounds. 6. Bake in the preheated oven for about 15 minutes, or until the edges are golden brown and the biscuits are set. 7. Remove from the oven and allow to cool on the baking sheet for a few minutes before transferring to a wire rack to cool completely.

NO-BAKE PEANUT BUTTER BALLS

These peanut butter balls are an excellent choice for anyone who desires a sweet snack without impacting blood sugar levels, ideal for diabetics or those following a low glycemic index diet.

RECIPE 2	NUTRITIONAL VALUES (PER SERVING, IF USING HONEY)			
Difficulty: Easy	**Calories:** 200	**Sodium:** 1000mg	**Protein:** 6g	**Sugars:** 8g
Servings: 1	**Fiber:** 2g	**Carbohydrates:** 12g		**Fat:** 16g
Preparation Time: 15 minutes	**Cooking Time:** 0 minutes		**Total Time:** 15 minutes	

INGREDIENTS	GUIDELINES
<ul><li>1 tablespoon natural peanut butter (unsweetened)</li><li>1 tablespoon ground flaxseed</li><li>1 teaspoon sugar-free sweetener (like stevia)</li><li>1/4 teaspoon vanilla extract</li><li>2 tablespoons rolled oats</li></ul>	1. Mix all ingredients in a bowl until well combined. 1. Form the mixture into small balls. 2. Chill in the refrigerator until firm, about 30 minutes

BAKED PEARS WITH CINNAMON

Baked Pears with Cinnamon is a deliciously simple dessert that brings out the natural sweetness of the pears with a touch of warming spices like cinnamon and cloves. This dish is perfect for a cozy night in or as a sweet end to a festive meal. The addition of a light sweetener enhances the pears' flavor without overpowering their natural taste, and the lemon juice adds a hint of freshness that balances the sweetness. This dessert is not only easy to prepare but also offers a healthier alternative to more decadent sweets, making it a wonderful choice for those looking to enjoy a guilt-free dessert.

RECIPE 3	NUTRITIONAL VALUES (PER SERVING, IF USING HONEY)			
Difficulty: Easy	**Calories:** 120	**Sodium:** 2mg	**Protein:** 0.5g	**Sugars:** 25g
Servings: 1	**Fiber:** 5g	**Carbohydrates:** 31g		**Fat:** 0.2g
Preparation Time: 5 minutes	**Cooking Time:** 25 minutes		**Total Time:** 30 minutes	

INGREDIENTS	GUIDELINES
<ul><li>1 large pear, halved and cored</li><li>½ teaspoon cinnamon</li><li>1 teaspoon honey or maple syrup</li><li>A small pat of butter or a drizzle of olive oil (optional)</li></ul>**Optional toppings:** a sprinkle of chopped nuts, a dollop of yogurt, or a scoop of ice cream	3. Preheat your oven to 375°F (190°C). Line a baking dish with parchment paper. 4. Place the pear halves, cut side up, in the prepared baking dish. 5. In a small bowl, mix the cinnamon, cloves, sweetener, and lemon juice. 6. Spoon the mixture over the pear halves, making sure each pear is well coated with the spice mixture. 7. Bake in the preheated oven for about 25 minutes, or until the pears are tender and the tops are slightly caramelized. 8. Serve the baked pears warm, possibly with a dollop of Greek yogurt or a scoop of vanilla ice cream for an extra treat.

PUMPKIN & SPICE MUFFINS

These Pumpkin & Spice Muffins are a delightful treat that combines the seasonal flavors of pumpkin with the warmth of cinnamon and nutmeg. Made with almond flour, these muffins are gluten-free and lower in carbohydrates than traditional muffins, making them an excellent option for those on specific dietary plans or managing blood sugar levels. They are moist, fluffy, and packed with flavor, perfect for a fall morning breakfast, a snack, or a healthier dessert option. Enjoy them on their own or topped with a spread of cream cheese for an extra indulgent treat.

RECIPE 4	NUTRITIONAL VALUES (PER MUFFIN, IF USING HONEY)			
Difficulty: Easy	**Calories:** 160	**Sodium:** 75mg	**Protein:** 6g	**Sugars:** 6g
Servings: 1 (makes about 4-6 muffins)	**Fiber:** 3g	**Carbohydrates:** 12g		**Fat:** 11g
Preparation Time: 10 minutes	**Cooking Time:** 20-25 minutes		**Total Time:** 30-35 minutes	

INGREDIENTS	GUIDELINES
<ul><li>½ cup all-purpose flour</li><li>¼ cup sugar</li><li>¼ teaspoon baking powder</li><li>¼ teaspoon baking soda</li><li>¼ teaspoon salt</li><li>¼ teaspoon ground cinnamon</li><li>⅛ teaspoon ground nutmeg</li><li>⅛ teaspoon ground cloves</li><li>⅛ teaspoon ground ginger</li><li>¼ cup pumpkin puree</li><li>2 tablespoons vegetable oil</li><li>1 egg</li><li>1 tablespoon milk</li><li>½ teaspoon vanilla extract</li></ul>	1. Preheat your oven to 350°F (175°C). Line a muffin tin with paper liners or lightly grease it. 2. In a large mixing bowl, combine the almond flour, cinnamon, nutmeg, baking powder, and salt. 3. In another bowl, whisk together the pumpkin puree, eggs, and sweetener until smooth. 4. Gradually add the wet ingredients to the dry ingredients, stirring until just combined. 5. Spoon the batter into the prepared muffin tin, filling each cup about three-quarters full. 6. Bake in the preheated oven for 25 minutes, or until a toothpick inserted into the center of a muffin comes out clean. 7. Remove the muffins from the oven and allow them to cool in the pan for a few minutes before transferring them to a wire rack to cool completely.

RICOTTA AND LEMON CAKES

These Ricotta and Lemon Cakes are a delightful dessert or snack that's light yet satisfying, featuring the creamy texture of ricotta and the bright, zesty flavor of lemon. The simple ingredient list and quick preparation make these cakes an excellent choice for a last-minute treat or a special addition to brunch. Their subtle sweetness and fresh lemony scent make them a favorite among those who prefer desserts that are not overly sweet.

RECIPE 5	NUTRITIONAL VALUES (PER CAKE, IF USING HONEY)			
Difficulty: Intermediate	**Calories:** 140	**Sodium:** 60mg	**Protein:** 7g	**Sugars:** 8g
Servings: 1 (makes about 4 small cakes)	**Fiber:** 0g	**Carbohydrates:** 10g		**Fat:** 8g
Preparation Time: 15 minutes	**Cooking Time:** 25 minutes		**Total Time:** 40 minutes	

INGREDIENTS	GUIDELINES
<ul><li>½ cup ricotta cheese</li><li>¼ cup sugar</li><li>1 egg</li><li>2 tablespoons unsalted butter, melted</li><li>½ teaspoon vanilla extract</li><li>½ cup all-purpose flour</li><li>½ teaspoon baking powder</li><li>Zest of 1 lemon</li><li>2 tablespoons lemon juice</li><li>Powdered sugar, for dusting (optional)</li></ul>	1. Preheat your oven to 350°F (175°C). Grease a 12-cup muffin tin with butter or oil. 2. In a large mixing bowl, combine the ricotta cheese, eggs, sweetener, lemon zest, and vanilla extract if using. Whisk together until the mixture is smooth and well combined. 3. Spoon the mixture into the prepared muffin tin, filling each cup about three-quarters full. 4. Bake in the preheated oven for 20 minutes, or until the cakes are set and lightly golden on top. 5. Remove the cakes from the oven and allow them to cool in the tin for 5 minutes before carefully transferring them to a wire rack to cool completely. 6. Serve the cakes slightly warm or at room temperature. They can be garnished with a sprinkle of powdered sugar or a dollop of whipped cream for an extra touch.

COCONUT FLOUR PANCAKES

These Coconut Flour Pancakes offer a delightful, health-conscious alternative for those looking to enjoy a sweet treat without the guilt associated with traditional pancakes. Made with coconut flour, these pancakes are notably low in carbohydrates and high in fiber, making them an excellent choice for people managing diabetes or adhering to low-carb diets. The inclusion of coconut flour not only imparts a subtly sweet, nutty flavor but also contributes to a satisfyingly fluffy texture, distinguishing these pancakes from their often-denser gluten-free counterparts.

RECIPE 6	NUTRITIONAL VALUES (PER PANCAKE)			
Difficulty: Easy	**Calories:** 200	**Sodium:** 100mg	**Protein:** 6g	**Sugars:** 8g
Servings: 1	**Fiber:** 2g	**Carbohydrates:** 12g		**Fat:** 16g
Preparation Time: 10 minutes	**Cooking Time:** 10 minutes		**Total Time:** 20 minutes	

INGREDIENTS	GUIDELINES
<ul><li>2 tablespoons of coconut flour</li><li>1 tablespoon of sugar-free sweetener (such as erythritol or stevia)</li><li>1/4 teaspoon of baking powder</li><li>1/4 teaspoon of ground cinnamon (optional)</li><li>1 large egg</li><li>1/4 cup of unsweetened almond milk</li><li>1/2 teaspoon of vanilla extract</li></ul>	1. In a bowl, mix the coconut flour, sweetener, baking powder, and cinnamon. 2. In another bowl, whisk the egg with the almond milk and vanilla extract until smooth. 3. Combine the wet ingredients with the dry ingredients, mixing well to avoid lumps. 4. Heat a non-stick skillet over medium heat and lightly grease with coconut oil or cooking spray. 5. Pour small amounts of the batter onto the hot skillet, cooking for about 2-3 minutes per side, until the pancakes are golden and cooked through. 6. Serve hot with a sprinkle of sugar-free sweetener or a serving of fresh fruit of your choice.

CHOCOLATE AND PEANUT BUTTER BARS

These Chocolate and Peanut Butter Bars are a decadent treat that combines the rich flavors of cocoa and the creamy texture of peanut butter. With coconut oil adding a slight hint of tropical flavor and a smooth consistency, these bars are not only delicious but also a healthier alternative to traditional sweets. Perfect for a quick snack, a post-workout treat, or a dessert, they offer a satisfying richness that can please any chocolate and peanut butter lover without the guilt of excessive sugars.

RECIPE 7	NUTRITIONAL VALUES (PER BAR, IF USING HONEY)			
Difficulty: Easy	**Calories:** 200	**Sodium:** 100mg	**Protein:** 6g	**Sugars:** 8g
Servings: 1 (makes about 4 small bars)	**Fiber:** 2g	**Carbohydrates:** 15g		**Fat:** 16g
Preparation Time: 10 minutes	**Cooking Time:** 0 minutes		**Total Time:** 10 minutes (plus chilling time)	

INGREDIENTS	GUIDELINES
<ul><li>¼ cup peanut butter (creamy or crunchy)</li><li>2 tablespoons honey or maple syrup</li><li>2 tablespoons coconut oil, melted</li><li>2 tablespoons cocoa powder</li><li>½ teaspoon vanilla extract</li><li>Pinch of salt</li></ul> **Optional:** 2 tablespoons chopped nuts or shredded coconut for topping **Optional toppings:** chopped nuts, sea salt, or shredded coconut	1. Line an 8x8-inch baking dish with parchment paper, leaving some overhang on the sides for easy removal. 2. In a medium mixing bowl, combine the peanut butter, cocoa powder, melted coconut oil, and sweetener. Stir until all ingredients are well incorporated and the mixture is smooth. 3. Pour the mixture into the prepared baking dish, spreading it out evenly with a spatula. 4. If using, sprinkle your chosen toppings over the top of the mixture. 5. Place the dish in the refrigerator and chill until the mixture is firm, about 1 hour. 6. Once firm, lift the parchment paper to remove the set mixture from the dish. Cut into 12 bars. 7. Store the bars in an airtight container in the refrigerator.

AVOCADO & COCOA MOUSSE

This Avocado & Cocoa Mousse is a rich and creamy dessert that offers a healthier alternative to traditional chocolate mousse. The avocados provide a silky texture and are a great source of healthy fats, vitamins, and minerals, while the cocoa adds a deep chocolate flavor without the need for added fats. This dessert is perfect for those who want to indulge their sweet tooth in a more nutritious way. It's a delightful treat that's quick to prepare and sure to impress with its luxurious texture and robust flavor.

RECIPE 8	NUTRITIONAL VALUES (PER SERVING, IF USING HONEY)			
Difficulty: Easy	**Calories:** 240	**Sodium:** 10mg	**Protein:** 3g	**Sugars:** 16g
Servings: 1	**Fiber:** 7g	**Carbohydrates:** 27g		**Fat:** 15g
Preparation Time: 5 minutes	**Cooking Time:** 0 minutes		**Total Time:** 5 minutes	

INGREDIENTS	GUIDELINES
<ul><li>1 ripe avocado</li><li>2 tablespoons cocoa powder</li><li>2-3 tablespoons honey or maple syrup (adjust to taste)</li><li>½ teaspoon vanilla extract</li><li>Pinch of salt</li></ul> **Optional toppings:** whipped cream, berries, chopped nuts	1. In a blender or food processor, combine the avocados, cocoa powder, vanilla extract, and sweetener. 2. Blend until the mixture is completely smooth and creamy. If the mixture is too thick, you can add a tablespoon of milk (dairy or non-dairy) to achieve the desired consistency. 3. Taste the mousse and adjust the sweetness or cocoa according to your preference. 4. Divide the mousse into serving dishes and refrigerate for at least 30 minutes to allow it to set slightly and become chilled. 5. Serve the mousse chilled, optionally topped with whipped cream or coconut cream, and a sprinkle of cocoa powder or chocolate shavings for an extra touch of elegance.

COLD CHEESECAKE WITH BERRIES

This Cold Cheesecake with Berries is a refreshing and lighter alternative to traditional cheesecake, perfect for a dessert that won't weigh you down. The light cream cheese provides a creamy texture without excessive fat, and the natural sweetness of the berries complements the richness of the cheese. This dessert is not only delicious and satisfying but also presents beautifully with its colorful berry topping. It's an ideal choice for special occasions or any day when you crave something sweet yet mindful of health.

RECIPE 9	NUTRITIONAL VALUES (PER SERVING, IF USING HONEY AND WITHOUT CRUST)			
Difficulty: Intermediate	**Calories:** 180	**Sodium:** 190mg	**Protein:** 6g	**Sugars:** 14g
Servings: 1 (makes 2-3 cheesecake cups)	**Fiber:** 2g	**Carbohydrates:** 18g		**Fat:** 10g
Preparation Time: 15 minutes	**Cooking Time:** 4 hours		**Total Time:** 4 hours 15 minutes	

INGREDIENTS	GUIDELINES
<ul><li>½ cup graham cracker crumbs</li><li>2 tablespoons unsalted butter, melted</li><li>4 oz cream cheese, softened</li><li>¼ cup powdered sugar</li><li>¼ cup heavy cream</li><li>½ teaspoon vanilla extract</li><li>Fresh berries (such as strawberries, blueberries, raspberries) for topping</li><li>Mint leaves for garnish (optional)</li></ul>	1. If using a crust, prepare it first by mixing crushed nuts or low-calorie biscuits with a bit of melted butter. Press this mixture into the bottom of a springform pan or pie dish, then chill in the refrigerator while preparing the filling. 2. In a small bowl, sprinkle the gelatin over the hot water and stir until the gelatin is completely dissolved. Set aside to cool slightly. 3. In a large mixing bowl, beat the light cream cheese until smooth. Add the sweetener, vanilla extract, and dissolved gelatin. Mix until well combined and creamy. 4. Gently fold in the mixed berries, being careful not to crush them if they are soft. 5. Pour the cheesecake mixture over the crust (if used) or directly into a pie dish or springform pan lined with parchment paper if going crustless. 6. Refrigerate the cheesecake for at least 4 hours, or until set. 7. Garnish with additional berries before serving.

DARK CHOCOLATE AND WALNUT SQUARES

These Dark Chocolate and Walnut Squares offer a rich and satisfying treat, combining dark chocolate's robust flavor with walnuts' crunchy texture. Coconut oil not only helps to blend the ingredients smoothly but also adds a subtle hint of coconut flavor that complements the bitterness of the chocolate. These squares are perfect for chocolate lovers looking for a healthier dessert option that's easy to make and enjoyable to eat. The high percentage of cocoa provides antioxidants, while the walnuts offer a good source of omega-3 fatty acids, making this dessert delicious and somewhat nutritious.

RECIPE 10	NUTRITIONAL VALUES (PER SEQUARE)			
Difficulty: Easy	**Calories:** 180	**Sodium:** 0mg	**Protein:** 3g	**Sugars:** 7g
Servings: 1 (makes about 4 small squares)	**Fiber:** 2g	**Carbohydrates:** 12g		**Fat:** 14g
Preparation Time: 10 minutes	**Cooking Time:** 0 minutes		**Total Time:** 10 minutes (plus chilling time)	

INGREDIENTS	GUIDELINES
<ul><li>½ cup dark chocolate chips</li><li>2 tablespoons unsalted butter</li><li>2 tablespoons honey or maple syrup</li><li>¼ teaspoon vanilla extract</li><li>Pinch of salt</li><li>¼ cup chopped walnuts</li></ul>	1. Line a small baking sheet or tray with parchment paper. 2. In a double boiler or a heatproof bowl set over a pot of simmering water, melt the dark chocolate together with the coconut oil, stirring continuously until smooth and well combined. 3. Once melted, remove from the heat and stir in the chopped walnuts, ensuring they are evenly coated with the chocolate. 4. Pour the chocolate and walnut mixture onto the prepared baking sheet, spreading it out into an even layer. 5. Refrigerate for at least 1 hour, or until the chocolate is fully set. 6. Once set, lift the parchment paper to remove the solid chocolate slab from the baking sheet and cut into 12 squares. 7. Serve immediately, or store in an airtight container in the refrigerator.

BONUS 1: MEAL PLAN 28 DAYS

Week 1 - Meal Plan

Day	Breakfast	Lunch	Dinner	Snack	Dessert
Monday	Tofu and Vegetable Scramble	Lentil and Vegetable Soup	Beef and Bell Pepper Stir-Frey	Spinach and Blueberry Protein Shake	Oatmeal and Apple Biscuits
Tuesday	Coconut Chia Pudding	Whole Wheat Pasta Primavera	Chicken Cacciatore	Carrot and Hummus Sticks	Baked Pears with Cinnamon
Wednesday	Cinnamon Oat Waffles	Grilled Chicken with Yogurt Sauce	Bean and Black Cabbage Soup	Seed and Nut Crackers	No-Bake Peanut Butter Balls
Thursday	Carrot and Walnut Muffins	Brown Rice with Shrimp and Broccoli	Mushroom and Spinach Omelette	Avocado Toast with Poached Egg	Pumpkin & Spice Muffins
Friday	Spinach & Avocado Smoothie	Baked Vegetable Pie	Sesame & Broccoli Tofu	Baked Zucchini Chips	Ricotta and Lemon Cakes
Saturday	Sweet Potato Croutons	Vegetarian Sandwich with Hummus	Turkey and Spinach Meatballs	Greek Yogurt and Berry Parfait	Coconut Flour Pancakes
Sunday	Mushroom and Thyme Omelette	Chickpea and Tuna Salad	Grilled Swordfish with Green Sauce	Cheese and olive Stuffed Cherry Tomatoes	Chocolate and Peanut Butter Bars

Week 2 - Meal Plan

Day	Breakfast	Lunch	Dinner	Snack	Dessert
Monday	Spelt and Pear Porridge	Whole Wheat Sandwiches with Smoked Salmon	Chicken and Vegetable Soup	Celery Boats with Peanut Butter	Avocado & Cocoa Mousse
Tuesday	Whole Wheat Blueberry Pancakes	Mediterranean Barley Salad	Shrimp and Vegetable Skewers.	Cinnamon Apple Chips	Cold Cheesecake with Berries
Wednesday	Homemade Energy Bars	Grilled Fish Tacos	Polenta with Mushroom Ragout	Oat and Chia Seed Bars	Dark Chocolate and Walnut Squares
Thursday	Carrot and Walnut Muffins	Turkey & Avocado Salad	Mixed Grilled Vegetables	Baked Zucchini Chips	Pumpkin & Spice Muffins
Friday	Cinnamon Oat Waffles	Baked Vegetable Ratatouille	Eggplant Casserole Parmigiana Light	Spinach and Blueberry Protein Shake	No-Bake Peanut Butter Balls
Saturday	Tofu and Vegetable Scramble	Vegetable and Quinoa Omelette	Corn Tortillas with Black Beans and Sauce	Cinnamon Apple Chips	Ricotta and Lemon Cakes
Sunday	Coconut Chia Pudding	Pumpkin and Ginger Cream Soup	Beef and Bell Pepper Stir-Fry	Carrot and Hummus Sticks	Chocolate and Peanut Butter Bars

Week 3 - Meal Plan

Day	Breakfast	Lunch	Dinner	Snack	Dessert
Monday	Spelt and Pear Porridge	Baked Salmon with Asparagus	Chicken Curry with Cauliflower Rice	Oat and Chia Seed Bars	Coconut Flour Pancakes
Tuesday	Coconut Chia Pudding	Vegetable & Coconut Curry	Bulgur Bowl with Chicken and Tzatziki	Celery Boats with Peanut Butter	Pumpkin & Spice Muffins
Wednesday	Cinnamon Oat Waffles	Minestrone Rich in Protein	Baked Cauliflower Steak	Cheese and Olive Stuffed Cherry Tomatoes	Oatmeal and Apple Biscuits
Thursday	Whole Wheat Blueberry Pancakes	Baked Cod with Tomato Olive Sauce	Crustless Vegetable Quiche	Avocado Toast with Poached Egg	Baked Pears with Cinnamon
Friday	Mushroom and Thyme Omelette	Tofu Buddha Bowl	Black Rice and Edamame Bowl	Greek Yogurt and Berry Parfait	Avocado & Cocoa Mousse
Saturday	Sweet Potato Croutons	Turkey & Avocado Salad	Lentil Burger	Seed and Nut Crackers	Cold Cheesecake with Berries
Sunday	Tofu and Vegetable Scramble	Pumpkin and Ginger Cream Soup	Mixed Grilled Vegetables	Spinach and Blueberry Protein Shake	Dark Chocolate and Walnut Squares

Week 4 - Meal Plan

Day	Breakfast	Lunch	Dinner	Snack	Dessert
Monday	Carrot and Walnut Muffins	Whole Wheat Pasta Primavera	Sesame & Broccoli Tofu	Celery Boats with Peanut Butter	Baked Pears with Cinnamon (p. 118)
Tuesday	Whole Wheat Blueberry Pancakes	Grilled Chicken with Yogurt Sauce	Polenta with Mushroom Ragout	Carrot and Hummus Sticks	Pumpkin & Spice Muffins (p. 120)
Wednesday	Spinach & Avocado Smoothie	Brown Rice with Shrimp and Broccoli	Bean and Black Cabbage Soup	Oat and Chia Seed Bars	Almond Milk Chia Pudding (p. 119)
Thursday	Spelt and Pear Porridge	Vegetarian Sandwich with Hummus	Turkey and Spinach Meatballs	Avocado Toast with Poached Egg	Ricotta and Lemon Cakes (p. 121)
Friday	Homemade Energy Bars	Chickpea and Tuna Salad	Grilled Swordfish with Green Sauce	Cinnamon Appe Chips	Blueberry and Lemon Sorbet (p. 123)
Saturday	Mushroom and Thyme Omelette	Baked Vegetable Pie	Lentil Burger	Greek Yogurt and Berry Parfait	Cold Cheesecake with Berries (p. 126)
Sunday	Cinnamon Oat Waffles	Baked Salmon with Asparagus	Shrimp and Vegetable Skewers	Seed and Nut Crackers	Chocolate and Peanut Butter Bars (p. 124)

This weekly meal plan provides a balanced variety of meals using the specific recipes you've outlined from your cookbook, ensuring a diverse and nutritious diet throughout the week. Each day includes different options for breakfast, two snacks, lunch, and dinner, providing variety and fulfilling nutritional needs.

BONUS 2: FAQS

Q 1: What foods should I eat regularly to manage my diabetes?

Answer: Focus on foods that have a low glycemic index (GI), as they help maintain blood sugar levels. These include whole grains, leafy greens, most fruits, nuts, seeds, and lean proteins. Incorporating a variety of these foods ensures you receive a balanced mix of nutrients while managing your blood sugar.

Q 2: Are carbohydrates bad for diabetics?

Answer: Not all carbohydrates are bad. The key is to select complex carbohydrates that digest slowly and have a minimal impact on blood sugar levels. Foods like whole grain bread, brown rice, and legumes are excellent choices. Avoid simple sugars and refined carbohydrates, which can cause spikes in blood sugar levels.

Q 3: Can I still eat sweets or chocolate?

Answer: Yes, but moderation is crucial. Opt for dark chocolate with a high cocoa content and low sugar. When craving sweets, go for natural sweeteners like fruits or small amounts of honey or maple syrup, and always account for these in your daily carbohydrate allowance.

Q 4: How often should I eat?

Answer: Eating small, frequent meals can help maintain a stable blood sugar level. Try to eat every 3 to 5 hours and include a good mix of protein, fats, and carbohydrates to keep your energy levels steady.

Q 5: Is fruit still allowed in a diabetic diet?

Answer: While fruit does contain sugar, it's natural sugar, which is far better than the sugar in processed foods. Fruits are also rich in fiber, vitamins, and minerals. Choose fruits with lower GI scores like berries, cherries, and apples, and always eat them in moderation.

Q 6: How can I make sure I'm eating the right portion sizes?

Answer: Learning to measure with common tools like measuring cups, spoons, and food scales can be very helpful. Visual cues can also be useful; for example, a serving of meat should be about the size of a deck of cards.

Q 7: What should I drink?

Answer: Water is the best beverage for managing diabetes. Avoid sugary drinks and limit caffeine and alcohol, as they can affect blood sugar levels. Herbal teas and sparkling water with a slice of lemon can be good alternatives when you want some variety.

Q 8: What are healthy fats, and why do I need them?

Answer: Healthy fats, such as those found in avocados, nuts, seeds, and olive oil, are essential for overall health and help absorb vitamins. They do not impact blood sugar levels and can help you feel full and satisfied. However, monitor the quantity as they are high in calories.

Q 9: How do I read food labels effectively?

Answer: Always check the total carbohydrates, which include starch, fiber, sugars, and sugar alcohols, on a food label. Look at the fiber content and deduct this from the total carbs for a more accurate carb count (net carbs). Also, pay attention to the serving size and sodium content.

Q 10: How can I dine out without sabotaging my diabetic diet?

Answer: Choose restaurants that offer hearty salads, grilled meats, and vegetable sides. You can request dishes to be prepared without added sugars or excessive fats. Don't hesitate to ask how the food is prepared and request modifications as needed.

BONUS 3: SUCCESS STORIES

Here, we share inspiring tales of individuals who have successfully managed their diabetes through dietary changes. These stories are based on real-life results, with fictional names and details added for privacy.

Story 1: James's Journey to Better Health

Location: Raleigh, North Carolina

Background: James, a 52-year-old high school teacher, was diagnosed with type 2 diabetes. He struggled with his weight and high blood sugar levels, despite being on medication. Success: After incorporating meals from the diabetic cookbook, James noticed significant improvements. He particularly enjoyed the "Whole Wheat Blueberry Pancakes" and "Vegetarian Sandwich with Hummus," which fit easily into his busy schedule. Over six months, James lost 20 pounds, reduced his HbA1c from 8.5% to 6.3%, and gained more energy to enjoy activities like biking and hiking with his family.

Story 2: Anita Finds Her Balance

Location: Boulder, Colorado

Background: Anita, a freelance graphic designer and mother of two, struggled to balance her diabetes management with a hectic lifestyle. Success: Anita started planning her meals using recipes from the cookbook, such as "Brown Rice and Salmon Bowl" and "Almond Milk Chia Pudding." She was able to stabilize her blood sugar levels and reduce her reliance on insulin. Anita's favorite part of her new diet was the variety and how it made her feel more in control of her health.

Story 3: Carlos Embraces Change

Location: San Antonio, Texas

Background: At 35, Carlos was a recent diabetic diagnosis who loved cooking but found it hard to give up his traditional, carb-heavy dishes. Success: By experimenting with diabetic-friendly recipes like "Lentil and Vegetable Soup" and "Shrimp and Vegetable Skewers," Carlos discovered new flavors that didn't spike his blood sugar. He successfully incorporated healthier versions of his traditional dishes and, within a year, significantly improved his lab results, impressing his doctor.

Story 4: Sarah's Sweet Victory

Location: Portland, Maine

Background: Sarah, a 28-year-old with gestational diabetes, feared for her baby's health and her own. Success: She used the cookbook to find sweet but safe treats like "Ricotta and Lemon Cakes" and "Dark Chocolate and Walnut Squares" to satisfy her cravings without harming her or her baby's health. Sarah continued these habits post-pregnancy, which helped her return to her pre-pregnancy weight faster and maintain her blood sugar levels.

Story 5: The Wilson Family Overhaul

Location: Fresno, California

Background: The Wilsons, a family where both parents and one child were diagnosed with type 2 diabetes, needed a family-friendly solution. Success: They adopted several recipes from the cookbook, making meal prep a family activity. Favorites like "Mushroom and Thyme Omelette" and "Pumpkin & Spice Muffins" became staples. This not only improved their health but also brought them closer together. Within months, all three saw improvements in their health metrics and overall well-being.

Made in the USA
Columbia, SC
14 July 2024

38619349R00041